Unlocking the Mystery
Christ Living IN You

Unlocking the Mystery

Christ Living IN You

Kenny Ashley

Unlocking the Mystery of Christ Living IN You
© 2018 Kenneth K. Ashley, Jr.

Please note that the author has chosen to capitalize certain pronouns that refer to the Father, Son, and Holy Spirit which may differ from some Bible publishers' style. The name of satan and related names are not capitalized. The author chooses not to acknowledge him even to the point of violating grammatical rules.

All emphasis added to Scripture quotations is the author's.

Published by:

Cover Design: Katie Butler, Daniel Hopper, and Joshua Hancock

ISBN: 9781729464526

Library of Congress

Table of Contents

Shout Outs!

To **Ben Rawls**. Ben has patiently driven me to write this book. Well, maybe not so patiently. He says I'm not getting any younger, so I better get to writing. He has been my friend, my encourager, and my confidant. He is always looking out for me. If not for God placing Ben in my life, I would not be in this place, at this time, writing this book, and doing and being what God has called me to be. Ben is a writer in his own right. His insights are scattered throughout the book. His passion to help people see that they are God's favorite is contagious and fervent. Thank God for you, Ben Rawls.

To **Daniel Hopper**. Daniel has a heart after my own heart. He 'gets it." He loves Jesus and people in a way that is inspiring. He loves kids and models for them what it looks like for Jesus to live in, through, for, and as us. He believes that the abundant life is 'caught,' not just 'taught.' He has an insatiable desire to help others 'see' Jesus as He truly is. God bless you, Hop.

To **Katie Butler**. Katie is my right-hand gal. She is such a blessing. There is nothing she cannot figure out if something goes awry. She fixes my computer (often). She creates and designs my PowerPoints and illustrations for the book. She handles all the publishing and formatting for my writing endeavors. She is really good at all this stuff. She is amazing. I could not do it without her. I wouldn't even want to try. Thank you, Katydid.

To my **JOurneY Church Family**. You guys are simply the best. You love me. And I certainly love you. You give me freedom to do what God asks me to do. You are true servants of the Lord. Thank you for accepting me and loving me just the way I am. Kinda like Jesus loves me. But then, Jesus is your life, too, right? Thank you, Lord, for the blessing of my JOurneY family.

About the Author

I know you are not supposed to put this section at the beginning of the book. However, I always like to know about the author before I read a book. I want to know who he is, and why he is writing. It helps me to know what he is passionate about and why. So, allow me to introduce myself.

Hi, I'm Kenny Ashley. I am guy who at one time had lost all hope of ever being happy. Today, I am a 'hope peddler' all because I finally came to realize that hope is not an emotion. Hope is a Person. Hope's name is Jesus, the Blessed Hope. A good friend of mine says that he is so happy his teeth dry out from smiling so much. Now, I understand what he means.

I'm also a Husband, Dad, Papa, Author, Conference Leader, and Pastor of The JOurneY at Lake Wylie, SC. I'm also an Awakener. I write books and devotionals, lead multiple Life Groups, and do everything I can to wake people up to the fact that God is crazy wild about them. My quest is to peddle Hope to as many people as possible before I stop breathing and go Home.

A.W. Tozer made a statement that has been the driving force in my quest to live full and free IN Christ.

He said, "What comes to your mind whenever you think about God is the most important thing about you."

This book elucidates how God changed my mind and my life, and what God is teaching me about His unconditional love and grace.

My goal is to encourage you to truly believe that you, too, are God's favorite. Every word you read is designed to help you see God as He truly is and to understand how He sees you. If we could ever understand how God sees and thinks about us, we would never be the same and life would be... WOW!

I send out *The Graceline*, my weekly devotional, to those who subscribe at www.kennyashley.com. It's free, quick, and easy.

You can also read my blogs and watch my videos anytime you need a little encouragement.

I teach a life-changing seminar called *LAY ASIDE EVERY WEIGHT.* To call it a seminar detracts from what LAEW really is. It is an intimate experience with the Lord in which He heals wounded spirits and broken hearts via the power of His Holy Spirit and forgiveness for oneself as well as one's offenders. Everyone needs to experience the transforming power of a LAEW conference.

I teach a conference on personality traits called *THE PEOPLE PUZZLE* which is a program of **Walk Thru the Bible**. It is based on the DISC profile and is a great tool for discovering how God wired you and how to better understand all of your relationships. Wanda and I also lead a marriage enrichment conference based on *THE PEOPLE PUZZLE* called *UNDERSTANDING THE LOVE OF YOUR LIFE.*

My Biographical JOurneY

At an early age, my belief system (my filter through which I see God, myself, others and life in general) was corrupted by THE lie of the enemy of our souls. THE lie is that God is not good and cannot be trusted. Because my faulty filter prevented me from seeing the truth of how much God really loved me, I believed that I was worthless, no good, and a disappointment to God because I could not be perfect enough to please Him. Since I could not please God, I tried to get all my emotional needs met through people. I became a people-pleaser par excellent. My pursuit of happiness via trusting people instead of God was a disaster. It led me down a road of misery and despair that I would not wish on the devil himself.

I grew up as an over-achiever both athletically and academically. I majored in pre-medicine because that's what other people thought I should do. But I didn't want to be a doctor. I wanted to be a coach. So after college I accepted a coaching job at my home high school teaching science and coaching football, basketball, and golf.

3

I started a chapter of the Fellowship of Christian Athletes teaching the Bible to young athletes. I taught them that God loved and accepted them unconditionally even though I didn't really believe it myself. The fact that many of them trusted Jesus and are still following Him to this day simply shows that the Message, not the messenger, is the key to life and life more abundantly.

After twelve years in education, I left the coaching profession and became a pastor. I thought God might love pastors more than coaches. As a pastor, however, I still lived in misery and depression due to my belief in THE lie about God.

Then one day, on July 22, 2007, God graciously opened my spiritual eyes and radically changed my filter. He allowed me to see how He sees me through His eyes of love, not condemnation. He transformed my life that day.

Once again, I find myself hopeless but in a wonderful way. I am hopelessly and helplessly in love with the Creator of the Universe… the One who created me just so He could love me and share His Life with me. It is a JOurneY. And JOY is in the JOurneY with Papa, our Heavenly Father, and with one another. I've discovered that we love God by loving people. And joy is always richer when it is shared.

MY FAMILY

I have been married at the time of this writing for 48 years to my Bride, Wanda, my high school Sweetheart and the love of my life. We have a son, Clay, and Megan, his Bride and our daughter-in-love. They have given us our first grandboy, Jackson. Clay is a real estate marketer. Megan is a registered nurse for a dialysis clinic. They live in Indian Land, SC.

We have a daughter, Kia, and John, her husband and our son-in-love. They are slightly ahead in the grandchildren race with three grandboys, Kai, Zane, and Bay. Kia is a physician's assistant in Charlotte, NC. John is a musician and worship leader.

4

Wanda and I live near Lake Wylie, SC only 40 minutes away from our grandchildren. Although we love our children immensely, we understand that one of the main reasons for their existence is to provide us with one of God's greatest treasures… grandchildren. We are so blessed!

MY CONTACT INFORMATION

You can contact me at <u>kennykashley@gmail.com</u> or follow me on Twitter @kennykashley, or on Facebook. You can also follow us on Facebook at The Journey at Lake Wylie. For access to my blog, vlog, sermon notes, and videos, go to www.kennyashley.com.

Dedication

To my GrandBoys.
Jackson, Kai, Zane, and Bay.
I call you my GrandJOYS.
Your Heavenly Papa gave you to your Papa
So I could see how much my Papa loves me.
Each of you is Papa's favorite.
Mine, too.

Guidelines for Reading this Book

I wrote this book thinking it was going to be the comprehensive treatise of **Christ IN you, the hope of glory**. The first time I wrote it, I used so much Scripture to prove my point that it was like reading Leviticus. Oh, it proved my point, but it was like eating a very lean steak that was full of protein but tough as nails with no fat in it at all.

Fat is what gives meat its flavor and satiation. Stories are to truth- telling what fat is to steak. It gives flavor to the truth. Flavor is what you remember. The shortest route from your heart to the truth is a story. Jesus was a master story teller. If this book was going to be about Him, it had to have more stories. More flavor.

So, I went back to the drawing board and wrote the book again. I rearranged some sections and added some flavor. I used Scriptural references for you to look up for more depth, but I illustrated the points more anecdotally.

I have written the book the way I talk. Therefore, it is not going to be grammatically correct. So all you lawyers and English teachers take a deep breath and just read. Understand that my goal is to communicate with you as if we were having lunch together discussing how wonderful it is that Jesus lives in us, through us, for us, and as us.

Our target audience for this book is religious people. I became one of those people when I was twelve years old. Religion is man's attempt to please God and earn His favor by performance, behavior, and keeping the rules. Religion is all about doing, not being. Religion told me that my worth was dependent upon how well I acted like Jesus.

My goal is to verify in this book that God has never wanted our obedience if He did not have our trust. What is about to be revealed to you is a life you may have never known was possible. Religion hid it from you. It did not want you to know the truth because the truth would set you free. Free from religion's control, manipulation, and guilt trips. God has set me free from that prison, and it is my passion for you to be free as well.

I capitalize parts of the Scripture to emphasize points I'm trying to make. We always capitalize any reference to God, including pronouns. We do not capitalize satan's name even though my word processor keeps yelling at me to do so. But I ain't gonna do it. Nope. he is not worthy of our even mentioning his name much less capitalizing it.

If you have been religious for some time, what you are about to read is going to require a major paradigm shift. Just read a little and let it soak in. Just take off your old lenses, keep an open mind, and ask Jesus to reveal the truth to you.

Believe me, there is nothing in this book that does not line up with Scripture. The Truth has always been right there in plain sight, but it has been distorted by the lens of religion. Hopefully what you read here will correct your vision so that you can see clearly how unconditionally Jesus loves you, and how crazy wild He is about you.

Whenever I go to a bookstore, the first thing that strikes me is this: What the world does not need today is another book. And here I am writing another one. My new found joy in Jesus compels me to do so.

My passion and my hope is that in these pages the Lord will awaken you to His love and grace so that you can enjoy life to the max with Him. He passionately desires for you to know and understand what is contained in these pages. I just hope and pray I don't get in His way.

Okay. Enough said. Let's get on with it.

Section One: The Mystery IN Jesus' Own Words

From Jesus' Own Lips to Your Own Heart

You were created to be ONE with Me. My Father chose you before the foundation of the world to be holy and blameless IN Me. I created the universe so that we could enjoy its wonders together forever. I so enjoy being with you.

I did not create you to live for Me. I created you so that I could live for you. You were never designed to live apart from Me. I am your life. I am your everything. You are the joy of My heart. The delight of My life. The apple of My eye. I love you more than you can ever imagine.

But in the beginning, humanity was deceived and took another route. Instead of depending upon Me for everything they needed, they thought they could make it without Me. Humanity lost its way and has been groping in darkness searching for its true identity in Me ever since.

Nevertheless, your heart still longs to be ONE with Me. I am the way back. All you have to do is to receive My gift of oneness with Me. It is your choice to make.

Religion has lied to you. Its rules and regulations can never make you ONE with Me. You cannot work to attain this gift. I alone can do this FOR you. I don't need your help.

When I said from the cross, "IT IS FINISHED!" I meant it. There is nothing... I mean nothing left for you to do except to trust Me and receive My life as yours.

Sin separated us. I created you to live in dependence upon Me. Sin drives you to act independently apart from Me. For you to become ONE with Me, your sin had to be dealt with.

I died on the cross to pay your sin debt. It is paid in full. All you have to do to receive complete and total forgiveness is to accept it.

How do you do that? A simple thank you is more than sufficient. There is no need for good behavior or performance on your part as a prerequisite for receiving MY gift. The minute you try to earn it, it ceases to be a gift. Your forgiveness is freely given just for the asking. I come to be your life by faith. The very act of receiving it proves that you trust what I am saying. Receiving is just another word for faith.

Forgiveness is just the first step in your becoming ONE with Me. You old sinful heart was damaged beyond repair. It was corrupted by sin. It was unfixable.

A Heart Transplant

Your heart (corrupted human spirit) was so defiled that I could not become ONE with it. You needed a heart transplant. I took out your old hard, stubborn, rebellious heart which gave rise to the sin in your life and replaced it with a new supernatural heart. As a matter of fact, I gave you My heart and put My Spirit in you so that we could truly be ONE together.

Once My heart is beating within You, we are literally fused together in a way that we can never be separated. Since I am fused with My Father and the Holy Spirit also, you are fused into ONE with all of us.

We love each other perfectly and unconditionally. And now you are loved the same way. Everything we experience, you experience as well. We are ONE. Together. Forever.

You might be wondering how you make all this happen. It is simple. For you to come and receive what We are offering, you simply choose to accept it.

Here is how you become ONE with Me.

"Lord, I believe what you are saying. I believe in my heart that You are all that you say You are. I accept You as My life. Live Your life in me, through me, for me, and as me. From this moment on, You are my Lord and Savior... my all in all. I surrender the stool of my heart completely to You. Thank You, for loving me to life."

The moment you choose to accept My gift, we are fused, united, and joined together forever. I take up residence IN you. I live in you. You live in Me. Simply trust Me to live in you, through you, for you, and as you. And I will. We will live and work together as ONE unit. Inseparable forever.

Many call this unity a mystery. Before we became ONE, you tried to live in your own effort and strength. You were consistently exhausted and confused because you were not created to live apart from Me.

Even after I become your life, you may still think that My life is something 'you' have to live. No. You cannot live My life. Only I can live My life. The mystery of Me IN you is that you can cease from your striving to earn what I want to freely give you. Your part is to trust Me. My part is to live and work through you.

When we become ONE, My past becomes your past. My present becomes your present. My future becomes your future. My life becomes OUR life, not just yours. We died on the cross as ONE. We rose from the grave as ONE. We now live as ONE. To the world, this is a mystery.

The truth is that you don't live anymore. I am now your life. As I am, so are you in this world. I live IN you. You can relax and enjoy the journey and leave the navigation to Me. You never heard the word 'relax' in religion, did you? You and me as ONE is a total mystery to the religious.

We are going to reveal this mystery to the world. You and Me together. Together. That is one of My favorite words.

Section Two: Everything He Is, We Are!

My First Religious Experience

Growing up, our family attended the First Baptist Church. One day when I was twelve years old, my Sunday School teacher pulled me aside and asked me if I had been saved. At that point in my life, what I heard him saying was, "Have you given your life to Jesus so you can go to heaven when you die?"

I responded, "No, sir, I haven't."

To which he responded, "Well, if you ever want to talk about it, let me know."

And he trotted on off to the worship service. It took a lot of guts for him to ask me because he probably didn't know what to tell me. That was the preacher's job, I guess. Nevertheless, that conversation started me thinking that I needed to 'get saved' because going to hell would be a real bummer for a perfectionistic people-pleaser.

All I knew about church was what I heard from the preacher. This is what my stinking thinking filter heard him say:

"Jesus died on the cross for your sins which are many. God hates sin and you are a sinner; therefore, God hates you, too. But Jesus loves you and took the punishment you had coming from God. He died in your place. Father God will let you into heaven because of what Jesus did for you, but He is not happy about it. You made Him kill His Son because you could not be perfect enough."

It didn't sound much like 'abundant life' to me, but if it would keep me out of hell, and there was no other way, then I knew I had better get saved.

The way you got saved in the Baptist church was to walk down the aisle at the end of the service while people were singing the invitation hymn. I believed that the only time you could get saved was on Sunday, and the only way to get saved was to walk the aisle and pledge allegiance to Jesus.

I spent the entire next week begging God not to kill me before Sunday. When Sunday came, I was ready. When they started playing the invitation hymn, three girls in my fifth grade class came trotting down the aisle and got saved before I had a chance to get out of the pew. I was certainly not going down there with those girls. People would think I was doing it because of them. I was not going to have them thinking that. So I spent another whole week begging God not to kill me until I could get back to church again.

Next Sunday came, and I was ready. The preacher said, "In conclusion..." and I was halfway out of the pew before the music ever started. I raced down to the front of the church, grabbed the preacher's hand and gave my speech.

"Preacher, I know I'm a sinner. I want Jesus to forgive me for my sins and take me to heaven when I die so I won't go to hell. Thank you very much."

The preacher was delighted. He asked me to sit down on the front pew until the hymn was over. Then he told the congregation that I had given my heart to Jesus and asked them to come down and 'fellowship' me into the church. My head was only bust high on some of those church ladies, and I almost smothered to death several times. I smelled like blue-haired ladies for two weeks, but I guess that was a small price to pay to miss hell.

When the preacher told me to sit down on the first row, I sat there for 16 years--- spiritually speaking. No one ever told me what had truly happened to me. No one told me that Jesus had come to live in me. That He had become my life. That I (the old me) no longer lived (Galatians 2:20). No one told me how much He unconditionally loved and accepted me. Nobody ever told me that I couldn't live 'the' Christian life. Nobody told me how crazy wild Jesus was about me just because I was His boy.

We had no youth group. No Bible studies. No discipleship classes. We just went to church on Sunday morning and were told to try harder to act like Jesus. Talk about an exercise in futility! Because I had a terminal case of 'stinking thinking,' I was enduring life, not enjoying it.

In spite of all this misinformation, God never gave up on me. As a matter of fact, He launched me on a new leg of our journey that would ultimately lead to the cure for my misery. And as one beggar shares with another beggar where he found something to eat, I want to share what He is showing me with you. Shall we?

What Does It Mean For Christ To Live IN Us?

Paul used the term 'IN Christ' over two hundred times in his New Testament writings. We were chosen 'IN Christ' before the foundation of the world, but what makes us true believers is the fact that we have invited Christ to come and live 'IN us.' We don't have eternal life because we do good things and act like Him. We have eternal life because He IS eternal life, and we are engrafted IN Him.

Therefore if any person is [engrafted] in Christ (the Messiah) he is a new creation (a new creature altogether); the old [previous moral and spiritual condition] has passed away. Behold, the fresh and new has come! (2 Corinthians 5:17 AMP).

First of all, our old previous spiritual and moral condition is gone, eradicated, as if it never existed. It has been erased. No evidence that the 'old us' was ever here. Wiped clean. No spots. No blemishes. We are holy and blameless just like God meant for us to be when He chose us IN Christ before the foundation of the world (Ephesians 1:4).

How can that be? Because Christ has become our life. Everything He was, is, and will be, we are. His past is now our past. His present is now our present. His future is now our future. We have a new identity IN Christ. As He is, so are we in this world(1 John 4:17)

Did Jesus have any sin in His past? No.

For we do not have a high priest (Jesus) who is unable to sympathize with our weaknesses, but we have One who has

been tempted in every way, just as we are — YET WAS WITHOUT SIN (Hebrews 4:15-16 NIV, capitals mine).

Since Jesus is our life, His past is our past. He had no sin in His past, and neither do we. There is no trace of sin in our 'new' life IN Christ. All our sin was in our 'old life.' What happened to it? Old things have passed away. Behold, all things have become new! Get your head around that!

When Jesus became our life, it is as if He has always been our life. We think God sees us as we 'were.' No! He sees us as we 'are.' And Jesus IS who we are, and He is all Papa God sees.

Do you think Papa loves Jesus? He loves you just like He loves Jesus because Jesus is who you are now. Do you think Jesus loves Papa? Of course, they are ONE, just as we are ONE with Christ.

I have loved you even as the Father has loved Me. Remain in My love (John 15:9 NLT)

We Are New Creations!

One of the great mysteries of nature is the metamorphosis of the caterpillar and butterfly. In the spiritual realm, the caterpillar represents our 'old self.' Our 'new creation' IN Christ is represented by the butterfly.

I'd like to share a story from Milt Rodriquez's book, ***The Butterfly within You: Understanding Your Identity in Christ.*** I highly recommend it to you.

Fred, the Caterpillar

Fred thought he was a worm. He was unaware of his real identity._Fred was not a worm. He was a caterpillar. Big difference. Worms don't have 'imagining discs.' Inside Fred's body was a seed of something totally different and more wonderful than Fred could ever imagine.

One day Fred looked up for some reason, and saw this expanse of blue. He asked a wise worm what it was. The wise worn said that it was called UP. Legend said there were creatures who lived and moved in the Big Blue Up. Fred became obsessed with Up.

Then one day, he met a beautiful creature on a blade of grass who told Fred that she was a FLYER. She told Him that he had the SEED of a flyer within him, too, and that he belonged in the UP.

It sounded too good to be true, so Fred returned to eating weeds. He still believed he was a worm. The first step in discovering your true identity is to know where you came from. Fred didn't know. He thought he came from worms.

When Fred, the caterpillar, was fully grown, he hung upside down from a leaf, and a chrysalis began to envelop him. His head turned skyward as if he sensed he was about to become a 'flyer' in the Big Blue Up. The curve of his body looked like a capital 'J.' Could it be that 'J' stands for something like, 'Jesus?' Fred's chrysalis was both a BRIDGE and a WORKSHOP. However, before he could be transformed into his true nature, a butterfly, Fred, the caterpillar, had to die.

FOR YOU DIED, and your life is now hidden with Christ in God. When Christ, WHO IS YOUR LIFE, appears, then you also will appear with Him in glory (Colossians 3:3-4 NIV, capitals mine).

Fred's chrysalis was a 'bridge' over which he would pass from being a caterpillar to becoming a butterfly. It was a 'workshop' in which the mystery of metamorphosis would take place. This transformation has astounded scientists for eons.

As he enters the chrysalis, Fred's 'imagining' cells begin to dissolve his digestive tract. Out of the soup emerges body parts and organs totally different from Fred, the caterpillar. A proboscis develops with which Fred, the butterfly, will eat nectar rather than weeds. Long spindly legs form which Fred, the caterpillar, never had. So will wings. Radically different eyes. A NEW creation altogether is constructed.

Caterpillars eat weeds. They are ground-bound. They have limited vision and mobility.

Butterflies fly in the Big Blue Up. They have wings and eat sweet nectar.

Now which one had you rather be? You were created to be a butterfly. God said so. Do you believe it?

The Seed of Christ

The land produced vegetation-all sorts of seed-bearing plants, and trees with seed-bearing fruit. Their seeds produced plants and trees of THE SAME KIND. And God saw that it was good (Genesis 1:12 NLT, capitals mine).

What would you think if you planted a tomato vine, and it grew avocados? Each plant and fruit seed makes a plant just like itself.

An orange cannot become a tomato because you slice it and put it on a ham sandwich. It is an orange because it came from an orange seed. A tomato is a tomato because it came from a tomato seed.

God placed the SEED of Christ IN us before the foundation of the world. That seed, just like all seeds, bears fruit of its own kind.

What would a Christ SEED bear? C.S. Lewis, one of the finest Christian minds of all time, says that we are 'little Christs.'

You might think that is blasphemy, but God's Word says it is true. We don't live anymore just as Fred, the caterpillar, does not live anymore. He is a butterfly. A brand new creation. We, the 'old us,' do not live anymore. Christ lives in us. We are indeed, 'little Christs' because we sprouted from His SEED.

One last thing before we leave this section. Fred, the caterpillar's DNA is exactly the same as Fred, the butterfly's DNA, although they look nothing alike. The DNA of an acorn is the same as the DNA as a hundred foot oak tree. A tiny sour apple's DNA is the same as the ripe, juicy apple's DNA.

We have the DNA of Christ. We may not look and act like Him right now, but we grow into His likeness as we keep walking in faith.

And so we are transfigured much like the Messiah, our lives gradually becoming brighter and more beautiful as God enters our lives and we become like Him (2 Corinthians 3:18 MSG).

I Must Decrease and He Must Increase

The moment we accept Jesus' gift of life, we get ALL of Him. Everything Jesus is, we become. He is our entire life. We don't need more of Him. He just needs less of us. A lot less. Say, 'none' of us.

He does not need our help. He delights in doing everything FOR us. Besides, Jesus said that without Him, we can do nothing (John 15:5). Can dead people do anything? No. They are dead. Remember we died, and now He lives in us, through us, for us, and as us.

However, our belief system needs to be re-programmed. We have been programmed by society, culture, and religion to be human 'doings,' not human 'beings.' We are taught to be 'independent.' To never depend on anyone. People will let you down. And they will. But Jesus will never let you down. Love never fails. God is love.

Even after He becomes our life, we still have trouble believing we are dead. Learning to give up control is a lifelong process. Besides, control is an illusion. We have about as much control over what happens in our lives as a leaf in a hurricane.

He is in control, but He will allow us to be in control if we want to be. When we find out how frustrating our 'control,' or lack thereof, can be, we begin to trust Him more and more. It is a journey. God enjoys the journey with us. As we trust Him, the journey itself becomes the destination.

That reminds me of a story.

I've got a Tiger in Me!

Suppose I take a golf lesson. The Pro watches my swing and agrees I need some lessons. He takes me into his office and shows me a video of Tiger Woods' swing. Then he tells me to go out on the course and swing like Tiger. Impossible, right? I cannot imitate Tiger Woods.

Suppose, however, that there was a way you could cut me open, and Tiger Woods was able to crawl inside me. Now, Tiger is living in me. I can hear him talking. Our conversation goes something like this:

"Hey, Kenny. You want to hit it like me?"

"You bet, Tiger. Let's do it."

"Okay. Let's grip it and rip it. Let me see what you got."

I grip the club, and Tiger tells me to move my left hand over to the right. It feels very uncomfortable. "Tiger, I don't grip the club that way."

"I know you don't, Kenny. That's why you hit it as bad as you do. Now, do you want to hit it like me, or not?"

"Okay. Okay. It just feels so unnatural."

"Now," Tiger says, "take your stance. Aim more to the right."

"No. No. No. I can't do that. I will hit it off the planet if I aim that way. That's not the way I do it."

Tiger is quiet. Finally, he says, "Tell you what. Why don't you just be limber, and let me take control. Just relax and let me swing for you."

It's difficult, but I relax and give Tiger control. He swings, and I experience what a perfect golf swing feels like. The ball mashes against the club face and launches three hundred yards straight down the middle. His power and grace flow through me effortlessly. Wow!

I think to myself, "If we can hit it like that with no effort on my part, how much better could we hit it if I helped him a little."

Tiger said, "Want to hit another one?"

"Oh, yeah!" But this time I try to help him. As I do, Tiger stops swinging, and 'I' miss the ball. Tiger says, "I don't need your help, Kenny. As a matter of fact, only one of us can swing. You get choose who that is going to be."

Just like the Tiger Woods' story, Jesus lives in you and me. Yes, His ways are not our ways and His thoughts are not our thoughts (Isaiah 55:8). And He doesn't need our help either. As a matter of fact, only one of us can have control. And we get to choose who that will be.

I can tell you from experience that my being in control has caused me to wind up in the rough on more than one occasion, just like some of my golf shots. It feels so unnatural to give up control. Nevertheless, I'm finding that when I get out of Jesus' way, joy and peace flow effortlessly through me like a Tiger Woods' tee shot.

No. I don't have a Tiger in me. I've got something better. They call Him, Jesus, the Lion of Judah. And He and I are swinging on the same plane.

Papa Living AS Jesus

When Jesus walked the earth, His Father lived His life through Jesus. Jesus was fully God and fully human. As a human, He had to set aside all His 'omnis.' His omnipresence (present at all places at all times), His omniscience (knowing all things), and omnipotence (all powerful). When He squeezed Himself in to a human body, He chose to limit His divine powers. As a human, He needed to remain connected and dependent upon His Father at all times so He could know what the Father wanted to do through Him.

Though He was God, He did not think of equality with God as something to cling to. Instead, HE GAVE UP HIS DIVINE PRIVILEGES; He took the humble position of a slave and was born as a human being. When He appeared in human form, He humbled Himself in obedience to God and died a criminal's death on a cross (Philippians 2:6-8 NLT, capitals mine).

If Jesus ever acted independently on His own rather that in dependency upon His Father, by definition, He would have sinned. That would have disqualified Him as our Savior, and we would have been lost forever. That is why satan was constantly trying to trip Him up by getting Him to act according to His own initiative. But Jesus never took the bait. Jesus depended totally upon His Father for everything at all times.

Jesus gave them this answer: "I tell you the truth, the Son can do nothing by Himself; He can do only what He sees His Father doing, because whatever the Father does the Son also does... By Myself I can do nothing; I judge only as I hear, and My judgment is just, for I seek not to please Myself but Him who sent Me (John 5:19, 30 NIV).

Now if Jesus can do nothing by Himself without totally depending on His Father, is there much hope that we can do anything without totally depending on Jesus? That's what I thought.

The Apostle John gives a vivid picture of Jesus' dependency and fusion with His Father in the fourteenth chapter of his gospel.

"Don't let your hearts be troubled. Trust in God, and trust also in Me. There is more than enough room in My Father's home. If this were not so, would I have told you that I am going to prepare a place for you? When everything is ready, I will come and get you, so that you will always be with Me where I am. And you know the way to where I am going."

"No, we don't know, Lord," Thomas said. "We have no idea where You are going, so how can we know the way?"

Jesus told him, "I am the way, the truth, and the life. No one can come to the Father except through Me."

Take, for instance, Siamese twins. Can one go anywhere without the other? Where one is, there the other is also. We are more fused with Christ than Siamese twins. Since we have become fused with Him, can we go any place where He does not go with us? Can Jesus go any place in which we are not with Him? That is why He does not 'show' us the way to eternal life. He IS eternal life. He IS the way.

"If you had really known Me, you would know who My Father is. From now on, you do know Him and have seen Him!"

Philip said, "Lord, show us the Father, and we will be satisfied."

Jesus replied, "Have I been with you all this time, Philip, and yet you still don't know who I am? ANYONE WHO HAS SEEN ME HAS SEEN THE FATHER! So why are you asking Me to show Him to you?"

"Don't you believe that I am in the Father and the Father is in Me? The words I speak are not My own, but My Father who lives in Me does His work THROUGH ME"(John 14:1-10 NLT, capitals mine).

In essence, this is what Jesus was saying to them:

"Listen, guys. The Father and I are one and the same. As I have lived here with you, it has been My Father doing His work in Me, through Me, for Me, and as Me. You see Me and think I'm doing the work. No, it's actually My Father living and working through Me."

Jesus Looks like You!

The Apostle Paul said, **"I worked harder than everybody, but it wasn't me. It was the grace of God working in me"**(1 Corinthians 15:10)

A few years ago a group of salesmen went to a regional sales convention in Chicago. They had assured their wives that they would be home in plenty of time for their Friday night dinner.

Well, as such things go, one thing led to another. The sales manager went longer than anticipated, and the meeting ran overtime. Their flights were scheduled to leave out of O'Hare, and they had to race pell-mell to the airport.

With tickets and briefcases in hand, they barged through the terminal to catch their flight. In their rush, one of the salesmen inadvertently kicked over a table which held a display of baskets full of apples. Apples flew everywhere. Without stopping or looking back, they all managed to reach the plane in time for their nearly missed boarding. All but one.

He paused, took a deep breath, got in touch with his feelings, and experienced a twinge of compassion for the girl whose apple stand had been overturned. He told his buddies to go on without him and asked them to call his wife when they got home to explain his taking a later flight. Then he returned to the terminal where the apples were all over the floor. He was glad he did.

The sixteen year old girl was totally blind! She was softly crying, tears running down her cheeks in frustration, and at the same time helplessly groping for her spilled produce as the crowd swirled around her. No one stopped to help her. No one cared about her dilemma.

The salesman knelt on the floor with her, gathered up the apples, put them into the baskets, and helped set the display up once more. As he did this, he noticed that many of them had become battered and bruised. These he set aside in another basket.

When he had finished, he pulled out his wallet and said to the girl, "Here, please take this $20 for the damage we did. Are you okay?"

She nodded through her tears. He continued on with, "I hope we didn't spoil your day too badly."

As the salesman started to walk away, the bewildered blind girl called out to him, "Mister..."

He paused and turned to look back into those blind eyes.

She continued, "Are you Jesus?'

He stopped in mid-stride, and he wondered. Slowly he made his way to catch the later flight with that question burning and bouncing around in his head: "Are you Jesus?"

Do people mistake us for Jesus? That's our destiny, is it not? For us to be a vessel... a vehicle... an earthsuit in which Jesus lives His life in us, through us, for us, and as us. There is a big world out there that is blind to His love, His life, and His grace. Many are battered and bruised like the little girl's apples. Will we slow down enough to notice them and allow Jesus to love them to life?

The salesman's encounter with the blind girl was not a case of 'mistaken identity.' It was a revelation of his true identity IN Christ.

Want to know what Jesus looks like? Look in the mirror. He looks like you. When Jesus becomes your life, He does not change your looks, your personality, your sense of humor, and your uniqueness. He personally knit you together in your mother's womb creating you just the way He wanted you to be.

Each and every one of us is a unique, one of a kind expression of His life and glory. Be who He created you to be.

He Is Living Water and I'm a Flavor

Think of it this way. I need to drink more water, but I like to taste it. So I have been buying those little squirt bottles that give it a little flavor. I like the lemonade and the southern sweet tea especially. Down here in the south, 'unsweet' tea is a contradiction in terms. We like it so sweet that it doesn't even need a glass to hold it up. Anyway, I digress.

Jesus is the water of life. I am just a flavor. Each and every one of us is a different flavor. Not everyone has the same taste. That is why God created us the way He did. Some people like lemonade, and the Lord draws them to me so He can quench their thirst for love through me and as me. If you are grape flavor, then He draws those who like grape to you so He can do the same for them.

Here is one thing you need to remember. We are not the water. He is the water. He alone can quench our thirst for Him. We are just the flavor. But once we are 'squirted' into Him, we become ONE with Him. We cannot be ever be separated.

In Jesus' prayer before He goes to the cross, He asks the Father to make us ONE with Him as He is ONE with His Father.

"My prayer is not for them alone. I pray also for those who will believe in Me through their message, that all of them may be one, Father, just as You are in Me and I am in You. May they also be in Us so that the world may believe that You have sent Me" (John 17:20-22 NIV).

Jesus is fused with the Father and the Holy Spirit. We are fused with Christ which means we are also ONE with the Father and the Holy Spirit.
On that day you will realize that I am in My Father, and you are in Me, and I am in you (John 14:20-21 NIV).

Do you realize right now that the God of the universe lives in you? And He has chosen to live His Life in you, through you, for you, and AS you.

Just let that soak in for a minute.

When Jesus walked the earth, Papa lived His Life AS Jesus. Now Jesus lives His Life AS us while we walk the earth! Whenever Jesus lives through us, people will think it is us, but we know better. It is really Jesus living AS us.

And that truth becomes even more mind-blowing.

"I tell you the truth, anyone who believes in Me will do the same works I have done, AND EVEN GREATER WORKS, because I am going to be with the Father" (John 14:12 NLT, capitals mine).

How in the world can we do greater works than Jesus? How does it get any greater than raising the dead?

Greater does not mean 'quality.' Greater means 'quantity.'

After Jesus went back Home, He sent His Holy Spirit to live IN us. I believe the Holy Spirit is the Spirit of Jesus without His earthsuit. Both are one and the same along with the Father. Each member of the Trinity all think exactly alike.

While Jesus walked the earth, He could only be in one place at one time. When He comes to live IN us, He lives His Life AS us. Now everywhere we go, He goes with us.

Just as Papa lived through Jesus, Jesus lives through us. That is why we can do greater (more) works. We are simply His vehicles through which He connects with people and loves them to life. Jesus can be in a lot of places at one time because all of God's children take Him with them wherever they go.

Like Father, Like Son

I was standing in the checkout line at Wal-Mart the other day behind a young dad and his seven year old son. They looked and acted like twins. They had on workout shorts, the same T-shirt, and both were wearing the same ball caps turned backwards. The son walked just like his dad. He talked just like his dad. He had the same mannerisms as his dad. They were like two peas in a pod.

How did that happen? For one thing, they shared the same gene pool. I'm sure the son shared some of the hereditary traits from his mom, but there wasn't much room left for her from what I saw. The son looked like his dad had spit him out of his mouth.

It is a simple rule of the universe: you become who and what you surround yourself with. You are a direct result of the thoughts that you think, the people that you spend time with, and the books that you read.

Therefore, if you want to 'change' your life, then you must 'change' your thoughts, 'change' the people that you hang out with, and 'change' the books that you read.

Spirit and Soul Are Entirely Different

We are a brand new creation in Christ. The spittin' image of Him. Our 'our old corrupted self' is dead, buried, erased, and gone forever.

You might say: "If that is true, then why do I keep having these bad thoughts and selfish desires? Why don't I feel and act like Jesus. I don't look or feel any different than I did before."

You need to understand that we are 'spirit' beings who happen to have a soul and a body through which we are able to live on this planet. We are not primarily a soul and body which just happens to have a 'spirit' attached to it. God's Spirit gives life to our spirit. The soul and body merely function to allow our newly created spirit IN Christ to express Himself to the world.

By one sacrifice He has made perfect forever those who are BEING MADE HOLY (Hebrews 10:14 NIV, capitals mine).

God is Spirit. Man is the only species made in the image of God. We are the only species that has a spirit that can be united with God's Spirit making us ONE with Him.

Being ONE with Him means that we are everything He is. Perfect. Complete. Whole. Holy. Lacking nothing. No, we can't run the universe, but we have His character. We are partakers of His divine nature (2 Peter 1:4).

He who unites himself with the Lord is ONE WITH HIM IN SPIRIT (1 Corinthians 6:17 NIV, capitals mine).

Our old human spirit was so corrupted after the fall that it was irredeemable. God had to give us a brand new human spirit that was compatible with His Spirit so that we could be fused, united, and joined with Him.

When God gave us a new spirit and fused us with His Spirit, we became ONE with Him IN SPIRIT. At that moment, we became the spittin' image of God... in our SPIRIT, but not in our SOUL.

The soul is the seat of our personality which is how God wired us to uniquely express His Life and glory to the world. And He gave you the personality He wanted you to have, so don't go trying to change it. Express it. Be who God created you to be. Don't let anybody talk you out of being you.

The SOUL is composed of three parts:

- Mind
- Will
- Emotions

The mind is not the same as your brain. Your brain is an organ of your physical body. It is like a computer. It just gives raw data. Your mind takes the raw data from your brain and interprets it.

Your mind can be deceived. Eve had the raw data about the poison fruit killing them, but satan deceived her mind into misinterpreting it. See what I mean? Do you see how what you think determines your destiny?

- Be careful of your thoughts, for your thoughts become your words.
- Be careful of your words, for your words become your actions.
- Be careful of your actions, for your actions become your habits.
- Be careful of your habits, for your habits become your character.
- Be careful of your character, for your character becomes your destiny.

The thoughts we think determine how our emotions feel. Feelings can be pretty persuasive with our will. Our will determines the course of action we take based upon what we think and how we feel. Once our will decides the course of action and initiates it, the body carries out the decision.

32

Our Soul is BECOMING like Jesus.

By one sacrifice, He has made perfect forever those who are BEING MADE HOLY (Hebrews 10:14 NIV, capitals mine).

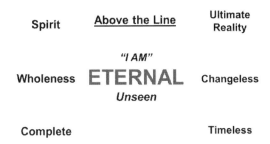

'Above the line' is the realm of the SPIRIT which has been made perfect forever in Jesus. It the realm of reality where our true identity IN Christ resides. It is the realm in which Jesus IS our life. Everything He is, we are. Complete. Whole. Changeless. Timeless. Eternal. Jesus is the same yesterday, today, and forever. He does not change. And neither does our spirit IN Him.

'Above the line' is the realm of the SPIRIT. It is the UNSEEN realm. It is the realm into which the soul only sees by FAITH.

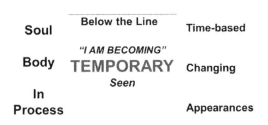

'Below the line' is the realm of the SOUL. It is in the process of becoming like Jesus in the spirit realm. The soul experiences 'mood swings' based on our situations and circumstances. Sometimes we feel good. Sometimes we feel bad. The way our soul feels does not determine the reality of our true identity in Christ.

'Below the line' is the realm in which we are BECOMING like we already are 'above the line.'

It is the realm bound by time. It is constantly changing and based on appearances. In this realm, our soul and body has not been redeemed and made perfect… yet.

God meant for it to be that way. We cannot see tomorrow. Faith is the evidence of things NOT SEEN. It is impossible to have faith in something we can see. God wants us to trust that He is already there in our tomorrow so we can stop worrying. Without faith, it is impossible to please God (Hebrews 11:6).

The Sermon on the Mount

I remember a cowboy, Lew Sterrett, who came to town with a ministry that involved training horses. He called it, *The Sermon on the Mount.* You know… 'mount' a horse. The pun losses its punch if you have to explain it. Anyway, God used Lew to illustrate true faith in a way I will never forget.

His horse was named Susie. They had been together for over ten years. He rode Susie around barrels and obstacles at break-neck speed. I thought it was amazing, but I hadn't seen anything yet.

Lew took off Susie's bridle, and then he blindfolded her. Yes, blindfolded her with no bridle. Lew directed Susie by shifting his weight and tapping her flank with his boot heels. Then he rode her over and around those same obstacles at the same reckless speed.

He finally rode her across the corral as fast as she could go. I just knew she was going to run smack dab through the fence. And then Lew leaned back, and Susie stopped on a dime! My jaw hit the top of my shoes! I was mesmerized. But what Lew said next was what really blew me away.

"Susie does not need to see where she is going. She knows that I know where she is going, and that is all she needs to know."

Here was a horse that trusted her life to her master, willing to go anywhere and do anything he desired. She never even flinched.

There I was balking and questioning the Master of the universe as if He had to let me 'see' what He was going to do before I would consent to let Him do it. Talk about a lesson in humility. I still need some plain old 'horse sense' when it comes to my walk of faith.

Is our true identity IN Christ ABOVE, or BELOW the LINE?

Above the LINE, everything Christ is, we are, too. He is our life. We are FUSED, UNITED, JOINED, and ONE with Him.

Can we SEE what is ABOVE the LINE? No. Why not? Because our life is HIDDEN with Christ in God.

For you died, and YOUR LIFE IS NOW HIDDEN WITH CHRIST IN GOD. (Colossians 3:3 NIV, capitals mine).

If we cannot see it, then how do we know it is true? By FAITH!

NOW FAITH is the assurance (the confirmation, the title deed) of the things [we] hope for, being THE PROOF OF THINGS [WE] DO NOT SEE and the conviction of their reality [faith perceiving as real fact what is not revealed to the senses] (Hebrews 11:1 AMP, capitals mine).

We live by faith, not by sight (2 Corinthians 5:7 NIV).

Let me ask you a question: Are you holy? Righteous? Perfect? Loving? Patient? Kind?

Is Jesus your life? If He is, then you are holy, righteous, perfect, loving, patient, and kind because Jesus is all those things whether you feel you are, or not. He is your true identity. Who He is, is who you are.

For us to be able to feel and experience the reality of our true identity 'above the line,' our thoughts must be focused on the truth of God rather than our feelings.

Since, then, you have been raised with Christ, set your hearts on things above, where Christ is seated at the right hand of God. Set your minds on things above, not on earthly things (Colossians 3:1-2 NIV).

Our Soul Swings like a Pendulum Do

Unlike our 'above the line' spirit IN Christ which never changes, the state of our soul changes with every thought. As the old Beatles song says, "It swings like a pendulum do."

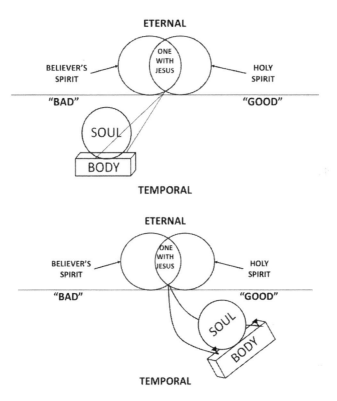

Our soul is affected by our circumstances, and we have no control over what happens to us. You can stand waist-deep in the ocean and think that a wave is not going to knock you over. However, in spite of all you do, you're still eating sand at the bottom of the sea.

One of the things we have no control over is whether our soul is going to be in a funk, or on top of the mountain. It is what it is.

God created us this way. Our soul is constantly fluctuating. One minute, you're in a good mood, and the next minute, you're in a funk.

The good news is that our soul does not determine our true identity in Christ. God's love and acceptance of me as a child of God is not dependent on whether I'm in a good mood, or a bad mood.

Sometimes we don't feel like Jesus. Sometimes we don't act like Jesus, but that does not mean that Jesus is not our life. So why did God create us with a soul that is constantly swinging back and forth from good moods to bad? Good question. Let's talk about that.

God is constantly trying to wean us off of our soul. If the only time we are going to trust Him is when we're feeling good, you better believe that the devil is going to try and make you feel bad all the time.

Remember, the state of our soul is dependent upon what we think. satan will give you a lot of things to think about that distract you from the awareness of your Oneness with Jesus. Sometimes he bowls you over with bad news. Sometimes the devil will plant a tiny seed of doubt in your mind. You worry about one thing then another, and before you know it, you've got a case of 'stinking thinking.'

Did I turn the water off in the bathtub? Did I pay that bill? Is my upset stomach cancer? A thousand little cuts. One won't kill you, but if you don't stop the bleeding, you will succumb.

That is why God tells us to take every thought captive and make sure it lines up with the truth. Whenever you have a thought that makes you feel down, ask the Lord if that thought has come from Him, or somewhere else. God wants us to depend 'souly and solely' upon Him every minute of every day.

We live in a fallen world with a soul created by the Lord. Our soul is constantly being altered by what we think. What we think determines how we feel. That's why God tells us to think about things that are true and honest and pure lovely (Philippians 4:8).

The devil will lie to us. He tries to make our thinking stink. That's why the Bible warns us to stop complaining (Philippians 2:14). Griping not only defiles us, it slimes everyone who has to listen to it. It leads to chronic 'stinking thinking.'

Stinking thinking leads to stinking feelings, which lead to stinking actions, which lead to stinking habits, which lead to stinking character, which lead to a stinking destiny. Stop griping! Barney Fife it. "Nip it in the bud!"

The devil tries to get us to believe that we are what we think. We are what we think only when what we are thinking is the truth. Jesus is the truth. Keep your eyes on Him. And don't beat yourself up when your soul gets out of whack. It is going to get out of whack until Jesus comes back. It is what it is.

If you're in a bad mood right now, get some rest. Go get something to eat. Go do something you love to do. Sooner or later, your mood will change. Wait for it. Don't make major decisions when you're in a bad mood. Keep resting in the Lord with all your heart and soul knowing that God is not disappointed in you because of your soul swings. Jesus had them, too, when he walked the planet, and He had no sin at all.

They went to a place called Gethsemane, and Jesus said to His disciples, "Sit here while I pray." He took Peter, James and John along with Him, and He began to be deeply distressed and troubled. "MY SOUL IS OVERWHELMED WITH SORROW TO THE POINT OF DEATH," he said to them. "Stay here and keep watch" (Mark 14:32-34 NIV, capitals mine).

Jesus never changes, but our soul is constantly in the process of change. Hang in there. One day we are going to experience fully our life IN Christ without the hindrance of a constantly changing soul. In the meantime, understand that you are a soul man, or woman, and don't get bent out of shape just because your soul does.

If Jesus had soul swings, you better believe that you will, too. Don't let the devil deceive you into thinking that 'good' Christians don't have them. Bullfeathers!

Renewing Our Mind

Notice in the diagram that the soul swing is anchored in Jesus. That anchor will hold no matter how the storms rage below the line. No matter how high the soul swings, Jesus is holding onto us. We are not holding on to Him. Rest in Him. Relax in Him. Keep trusting in Him. Fix your mind on Him.

Jesus gave us a new heart. A new spirit. Our old corrupt spirit is gone, but He did not give us a new soul. The soul still functions under the old, default operating system. A system in which 'self' was the source of meeting our needs rather than the Lord.

Yes, He gave us a brand new operating system. A radically different, supernatural spirit. The old independent spirit is gone, but the soul continues the think, feel, and act as if the old system is still operational. It must learn to trust the new spirit's operating system. And that can take some time.

A young boy sat next to his abusive, mean-spirited father at the dinner table. The boy was deathly afraid of his dad. He was so nervous when dinner time came, he spilled his drink at every meal. Whenever he did, his dad would backhand him and tell him how %#*@ stupid he was.

One day, his dad died. That night at supper, the boy reached up to get his drink and knocked it over. And when he did, he ducked to avoid the backhand even though his father was not there. It took a while for him to overcome the fear of spilling his drink although his dad was dead and gone.

The Principle of Thought

Do you know how many thoughts you have each and every day? Over 50,000 thoughts. No wonder God has so much to say about how we think.

As a man THINKS in his heart, so is he...Proverbs 23:7 KJV capitals mine

For the rest, brethren, whatever is true, whatever is worthy of reverence and is honorable and seemly, whatever is just, whatever is pure, whatever is lovely and lovable, whatever is kind and winsome and gracious, if there is any virtue and excellence, if there is anything worthy of praise, think on and weigh and take account of these things [fix your minds on them] (Philippians 4:8 AMP).

What you THINK is a big deal. If thinking right things is automatic, why does God tell us in the Bible what to fix our minds upon? All that you achieve and all that you fail to achieve is the direct result of your own thoughts.

Every negative and positive feeling is a direct result of thought. Whether you are angry... depressed... jealous... happy... sad... glad... etc. is a result of your thoughts.

We are the producers of our thoughts! Thought is not something that happens to us, but something we do. We have the power to choose what we think about. So we must choose our thoughts carefully because what we THINK determines what we see... not the other way around. Seeing is NOT believing. Believing (thought) is seeing.

Our THINKING, not our circumstances, determines how we feel and how we SEE life. It's easier to blame our unhappiness on what happens to us rather than our thinking.

Thinking is an ability, not reality. What you think is not necessarily reality. It's just what you think about it. An outside circumstance itself is neutral. What you think about it gives it meaning. That's why the same circumstance will mean entirely different things to different people.

41

The Pony in the Manure Pile

My two favorite Presidents were Abraham Lincoln and Ronald Reagan. Both were master story tellers. Both used stories to convey their messages and get their points across. So did Jesus... the Master Story Teller. Anthony de Mello says that the shortest distance between the truth and the heart is a story. Please allow me to share one of President Reagan's favorites.

There once was a pair of twins. Worried that the boys had developed extreme personalities — one was a total pessimist, the other a total optimist — their parents took them to a psychiatrist.

First, the psychiatrist treated the pessimist. Trying to brighten his outlook, the psychiatrist took him to a room piled to the ceiling with brand-new toys. But instead of yelping with delight, the little boy burst into tears.

"What's the matter?" the psychiatrist asked, baffled. "Don't you want to play with any of the toys?"

"Yes," the little boy bawled, "but if I did I'd only break them."

Next the psychiatrist treated the optimist. Trying to dampen his outlook, the psychiatrist took him to a room piled to the ceiling with horse manure. But instead of wrinkling his nose in disgust, the optimist emitted just the yelp of delight the psychiatrist had been hoping to hear from his brother, the pessimist. The optimist clambered to the top of the pile, dropped to his knees, and began gleefully digging out scoop after scoop with his bare hands.

"What do you think you're doing?" the psychiatrist asked, just as baffled by the optimist as he had been by the pessimist.

"With all this manure," the little boy replied, beaming, "there must be a pony in here somewhere!"

Recently I watched a program that told the story of 42 year-old Chris Rosati. Chris was diagnosed with *amyotrophic lateral sclerosis* (ALS, or more commonly called, Lou Gehrig's disease). It is a disease in which the motor neurons in the brain and spinal cord deteriorate and are unable to send messages to the muscles. Eventually the muscles atrophy from lack of use and ultimately lead to death. There is no known cure.

Having received a death sentence upon diagnosis of ALS, most people would fall into depression and waste away, but not Chris. He concocted a wild scheme to steal a Krispy Kreme donut truck and ride around giving away donuts. He wanted to be like Robin Hood, stealing cholesterol from the rich and giving it to the poor.

Chris said one of the blessings of having ALS is that he had nothing to lose. "What are they gonna do? Arrest me?"

Krispy Kreme learned of the plot and brought Chris a huge bus filled with donuts. They spent the day on this rolling sugar-high stopping at parks, cancer wards, and children's hospitals. They ended their journey at Chris' old high school passing out smiles and donuts to everyone.

Chris said that if dying has taught him anything it is how to live. Life is like a donut. You only go around once, and you have to make people smile while you still have the chance. He said if he could not use his lot in life to positively impact people, then the whole thing was a waste.

Chris found his pony in the midst of his manure pile. Are you going to let the stench of yours drive you to despair, or are you going to start digging? There's gotta be a pony in there somewhere! And that's the *hole* truth, and nothing but the truth!

Flesh: The Residue of the Old Self

Our 'old self-centered, Adamic nature' is gone. He is never coming back. But if we don't think he's gone, then he still exists in our thoughts. If he does, then we will continue to live and act as if our 'old self' is still in control. That's why we must focus our thoughts on the truth as revealed to us by His Spirit.

The FLESH is the residue of the 'old self.' The flesh is what the boy remembers about his dad who backhanded him when he spilled his drink. His dad is gone, but he still acts as if he is alive. His mind and ours must be renewed to match the mind of Christ. And we do have the mind of Christ.

The FLESH is sense and reason apart from reliance upon the Holy Spirit. It is independent to the core. It will never surrender control to God and depend upon Him for anything.

Whether we fix our thoughts on the FLESH, or on the SPIRIT, is a matter of life and death.

For those who are according to the FLESH set their minds on the things of the FLESH, but those who are according to the Spirit, the things of the Spirit. For the mind set on the FLESH is death, but the mind set on the Spirit is life and peace, because the mind set on the FLESH is hostile toward God; for it does not subject itself to the law of God, for it is not even able to do so; and those who are in the FLESH cannot please God (Romans 8:5-9 NASB, capitals mine)

Our mind must come into line with the mind of Christ. In order for that to happen, our mind must be renewed. Remember, we did not get a new mind when our spirit was made new forever in Christ.

Don't copy the behavior and customs of this world, but LET GOD TRANSFORM YOU INTO A NEW PERSON BY CHANGING THE WAY YOU THINK. Then you will learn to know God's will for you, which is good and pleasing and perfect (Romans 12:2 NLT, capitals mine).

As We Think, We Are… (Proverbs 23:7 KJV).

44

Points to Ponder

- Jesus is our life. We don't live anymore.
- We are spiritual beings with a soul and a body (earthsuit), not a physical being with a spirit.
- We are completely new creations. We are no longer 'sinners saved by grace.'
- There is nothing sinful about us IN Christ. The Bible calls us 'saints.'
- Everything He is, we are. We are holy and righteous IN Him because He is our life now.
- Our soul and body are vessels and vehicles through which He lives His life in this world.
- We choose to let Him live in us, through us, for us, and as us.
- Or we choose to remain in control and live according to the 'flesh' if we so desire. It's our choice.
- We will never be able to live past what we believe.
- If what we believe is a lie, it will negatively affect what we think, how we behavior, and the choices we make.
- It is imperative that we believe the truth about who we are IN Christ.

Section Three: The Mystery Revealed!

Preface: The Truth Will Set You Free!

In this section, we will understand more clearly that we who have been united with Him are ONE spirit IN Him (1 Corinthians 6:17). We are fused together with Him. One and the same with Him. No, we are not God, but we are partakers of His divine nature (2 Peter 1:4).

In the spirit realm, we have been forever made perfect IN Him. Our soul, however, has not been made perfect… yet. Our spirit is ONE with Him and therefore sees and thinks just like He does. Our soul can only see with faith eyes.

How was Peter able to walk on the water? Jesus told him to come out to Him. Peter believed Him. How do we know Peter believed what Jesus said? Because he got out of the boat!

Just like Peter, the Lord is going to reveal the truth to you. The truth is that Jesus became your life when you trusted Him by faith and received His grace. Grace is what God does FOR you.

We will see how God delights in living His Life in us, through us, for us, and as us. Jesus says that without Him, we can do nothing (John 15:5). But we can do all things 'through' Him who gives us His strength.

We will see that experiencing the Life of Christ in our soul takes time and faith. As we keep trusting Him minute by minute, we will begin to feel and experience His love, joy, peace, patience, gentleness, goodness, faithfulness, meekness, and self-control in our soul.

Many abandon their faith walk too soon. Why? Because we have been programmed to LEARN and then DO. "Teach me how to do it, and then I will go out and do it."

I hear this from people all the time. "Kenny, I think I got it. Jesus is my life. He wants to live His life in me, through me, for me, and as me. Now, tell me how to DO that."

We don't DO that. That is Jesus' part. He does the doing. We provide the faith. God's Word is a true, but you will never experience it until you believe it… cling to, trust in, rely upon, and put your whole weight upon it.

What you will come to understand in this section is going to astound you with its simplicity. You simply entrust the control of your life to Him. He will do the rest FOR you.

This life IN Christ is simple, but not easy. We all have been programmed to learn and do. Now you are going to learn to let Jesus DO FOR you. Giving up control is not an easy task, but it's a piece of cake for Jesus. You simply ask Him to take control FOR you, because you cannot give it up on your own. The flesh will never let go on its own and without a fight. You cannot fight the flesh. Jesus has to do that FOR you. Simply ask Him.

Question is: Will you let Jesus live for YOU?

What you are about to read will radically transform your life. Proceed with reckless abandon. Throw caution to the wind. You are about to embark on the adventure of a lifetime!

Okay, let's step out into the water and wade out a little bit deeper!

Christ IN You, the Hope of Glory

God has chosen to make known among the Gentiles the glorious riches of this mystery, which is CHRIST IN YOU, the hope of glory (Colossians 1:27 NIV, capitals mine).

Points to Ponder

- God chose us IN Christ before the foundation of the world.
- There were two trees in the Garden of Eden.
- Adam and Eve were IN Christ up until the fall.
- Although Adam and Eve were IN Christ, Jesus was not IN them.

God chose us IN Christ before the foundation of the world and ordained that we be holy and blameless IN Him.(Ephesians 1:4 NIV).
Our true identity IN Christ is based on our BIRTH, not our BEHAVIOR. If you can understand this truth, you will understand the Bible in ways you never thought possible.

Jesus told Nicodemus, **"You must be born again"** (John 3:7).

If you are a child of God, you have the nature of God within you. You will naturally behave and act as God would because He will live His life IN you if your soul surrenders to His control. Simple, but your soul loves to be in control. Making it surrender is the hard part. Let Jesus do that FOR you, too.

If you are not a child of God, it is impossible to behave and act like Jesus because you do not have His nature. According to the Bible, your 'ungodly' nature is antithetical to God. It abhors holiness. It loves independence and being in control. Besides , your 'old self' is dead because it is severed from the Life of Christ who is the Source of all life. Dead people can act at like anything, especially Jesus.

For example, a pig loves mud. Pigs have no sweat glands and have great difficulty keeping their bodies cool. The mud holds

49

moisture longer than water by itself. They don't mind being dirty if it keeps them cool.

Cats on the other hand hate mud and dirt. They constantly clean themselves with their tongues. They despise being dirty.

Pigs and cats have entirely different natures. You won't find a cat wallowing in a mud hole, and you will never find a pig licking himself clean.

God designed us to be holy and blameless IN Christ Jesus. Can we ever be holy and blameless in our behavior without His nature? No.

The Bible tells us that all have sinned and fall short of the glory of God (Romans 3:23). We are born with a sinful nature. We are born disconnected from God, the Source of our life. Sin. Acting independently on our own separates us from Him. Sin is the nature of fallen man.

The only way we can be holy and blameless is IN Jesus. As children of God, we are holy and blameless because He is our life. Jesus hates sin. He does not hate us, but He hates sin because it separates us from Him (1 John 4:17).

God's one desire has always been to live in union with us. We were created to be His children. He wanted to invite us to be part of His family: the Father, the Son, and the Holy Spirit. He wanted us to experience the same love that each member of the Trinity enjoys with one another.

Therefore, since it pleased God that the Trinity in His fullness would dwell in the body of Christ, He placed us IN Him before the world began. We were children of God way before we ever became human children.

Adam and Eve Were IN Christ Up Until the Fall.

In the beginning, God created everything in six days. Whether that is six twenty-four-hour days, or six time periods, is yours to decide. Nevertheless, every time God created something, He would say, **"It is good."**

On the sixth day, God looked over all that He had created.

Then God said, "Let US make man in OUR image, according to OUR likeness (Genesis 1:26 NKJV, capitals mine).

Note the Family talk: Let US... In OUR image. God is a Family. To be made in God's image is to be part of a family. God's nature is communal. 'Together' is one of His favorite words.

God does not exist as an individual. He is ONE God, but He exists as THREE Persons. He did not create us to be isolated individuals either. God is relational. As His children, we are wired for relationship, too. Relationship with God and with people.

So God gathered up some dirt and fashioned it into a human male. Then He breathed into his nostrils the breath of life, and the human became a living being. He called him, Adam, which means 'mankind.'

After He created Adam, He said that something was 'not good.' He said it was 'not good' for the man to be alone. So He put Adam to sleep and opened his side. He took one of Adam's ribs and made a woman.

When Adam woke up, there was this gorgeous being standing in front of him. Adam said, "WHOA! MAN!" And that gorgeous being has been called 'WO-MAN' ever since.

I thought you might be getting a little too serious, so I thought I'd lighten things up a bit. Okay, where were we?

Take note. Eve was not created. She was IN Adam. She was taken out of Adam. She was made from Adam's rib, which means she had the same DNA as Adam. She had his very nature.

When Adam loved her, he was, in essence, loving himself. When Eve loved Adam, she was loving herself. They were ONE just as God is ONE existing as THREE Persons.

We love God by loving people. If Christ is your life, when I love you, I am really loving Jesus. Neat, huh?

We were IN Christ before the foundation of the world. We are the Bride of Christ. We came out of Jesus side when He died on the cross just as Eve, Adam's bride, came out of him. When the Roman soldier pierced Jesus' side when He was on the cross, blood and water flowed out.

Jesus answered, "I tell you the truth, no one can enter the kingdom of God unless he is born of water and the Spirit (John 3:5-6 NIV).

It is the Spirit that gives life. Scripture tells us that life is in the blood. Water represents cleansing. On the cross, Jesus' Bride (all born again children of God) came out of His side. We have His blood flowing through our veins. We have the same DNA as Jesus. We have His very nature. He becomes our Life when we, by faith, ask Him to be.

There Were Two Trees in The Garden.

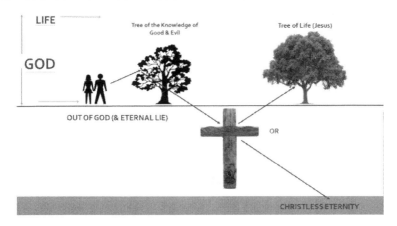

There were two trees in the Garden of Eden. One was called the tree of the knowledge of good and evil. Its fruit was poison. It was like **RoundUp**. Its fruit killed completely down to the very root of life.

The other tree was called the Tree of Life. This Tree was Jesus, the Source of all Life. It was like **MiracleGro**. Its fruit gave life eternally and abundantly.

Adam could have eaten the fruit of either tree, but he chose poorly. He chose knowledge instead of life... Jesus' life. Had he eaten from the Tree of Life, Jesus would have entered INTO Him, and Adam would have lived forever because Jesus would have become his life, and Jesus IS eternal life.

Before they ate the poison fruit, Adam and Eve were IN God. After they ate the poison fruit, they were disconnected from Him. They chose to live independently outside of God's control and influence. Their poor choice put them on a trajectory that took mankind farther and farther away from God's life. There was only one way to stop the fall and reroute man back in to the life of God. The CROSS.

The cross requires that we humble ourselves and invite Jesus INTO us. Until Jesus comes to live IN us, we are IN Christ, but He is still on the outside looking in. We are still in control of our lives. We are still sitting on the stool of our heart running the show.

Remember: The mystery that was hidden for ages is now revealed. The mystery is Christ IN us, the hope of glory. Man has been IN Christ, but Christ has not been IN him. Not until we receive Him by faith.

'Receive' is another word for faith. If Jesus has the supply for every need we have, the act of receiving it from Him verifies our faith.

When we accept the terms of the cross, it deflects us back INTO God where we receive His gift: Jesus, Himself, who is eternal life. The terms of the cross is absolute surrender. Completely giving up control of our lives as Jesus surrendered control of His life to His Father when He took up His cross.

When we eat the fruit of the Tree of Life, Christ comes to live IN us as we have lived IN Him.

At that day you will know that I am in My Father, and you in Me, and I in you (John 14:20-21 NKJV).

Adam and Eve, however, chose to eat the poison fruit and was deflected OUT of the life of Christ. Here is how it went down.

The Lord God took the man and put him in the Garden of Eden to work it and take care of it. And the Lord God commanded the man, "You are free to eat from any tree in the garden; but you must not eat from the tree of the knowledge of good and evil, for when you eat of it you will surely die" (Genesis 2:15-17 NIV).

Why would eating the fruit of this tree cause death?

For the wages of sin is death (Romans 6:23 NIV).

As for you, you were dead in your transgressions and sins (Ephesians 2:1 NIV).

The middle letter in S-I-N is 'I.' Sin is when I act independently in my own strength and wisdom rather than in dependence upon God. Sin engulfs me when I am the source of my life instead of God. I can even do 'good' stuff, and it still is considered sin

54

because I did independently on my own. Think of the Pharisees of Jesus' day.

Sin is SELF-centered rather than OTHER-centered. Anything that originates from self as its source rather than God as the Source is sin.

Jesus called the religious establishment of His day a 'brood of vipers' and 'white-washed tombs full of dead men's bones.' Why? Because they were SELF-righteous. Their righteousness did not originate from God as the Source, but from their own self-righteous deeds.

So what happened to Adam and Eve that caused them to become separated from God? We find the answer in the third chapter of the Book of Genesis.

The serpent was the shrewdest of all the wild animals the Lord God had made. One day he asked the woman, "Did God really say you must not eat the fruit from any of the trees in the garden?"

Did you notice that the serpent 'singled' out the woman? He did not talk to Adam and Eve together although Adam was standing right there beside her. He approached her as an 'individual.' He told her that she could be like God 'by herself.' That is impossible. God is not an individual. He is a community. He is a family. He is relational. He is love. It is impossible to love without someone to love. She cannot be made in the image of God by herself. God's nature is communal.

"Of course we may eat fruit from the trees in the garden," the woman replied. "It's only the fruit from the tree in the middle of the garden that we are not allowed to eat. God said, 'You must not eat it or even touch it; if you do, you will die.'"

Did God tell them not to touch it? No, He did not. How could they tend the Garden and not touch it? I believe this is the first vestige of religion.

Religion is man's attempt to gain God's favor by keeping the rules. Religion adds more rules to the Word of God. God is not very pleased with that.

I warn everyone who hears the words of the prophecy of this book: If anyone adds anything to them, God will add to him the plagues described in this book. And if anyone takes words away from this book of prophecy, God will take away from him his share in the tree of life and in the holy city, which are described in this book (Revelation 22:18-19 NIV).

Grace is what God does FOR us. We are saved by grace through faith which is simply trusting what God says is true. The moment we add anything to it, it ceases to be grace. Remember, God didn't create us to live FOR Him. He created us so He could live FOR us.

"You won't die!" the serpent replied to the woman. "God knows that your eyes will be opened as soon as you eat it, and you will be like God, knowing both good and evil."

Excuse me. Didn't God say that if they ate the fruit they would die? satan is a liar. Jesus called him the father of lies.

Take note that satan is speaking to Eve's soul. The soul is comprised of our mind, will, and emotions. He first attacks her mind with a probe of doubt. "Did God really say you would die?"

The mind is the battlefield of the soul. If he can get Eve to doubt in her mind the truth of God, then it is a short leap to her willfully taking action to eat the fruit. Once she started thinking how wonderful it would be to be like God, her emotions kicked in, and she started to desire the fruit.

The woman was convinced. She saw that the tree was beautiful and its fruit looked delicious, and she wanted the wisdom it would give her. So she took some of the fruit and ate it. Then she gave some to her husband, who was with her, and he ate it, too.

At that moment their eyes were opened, and they suddenly felt shame at their nakedness. So they sewed fig leaves together to cover themselves (Genesis 3:1-7 NLT).

Do you remember when God brought Adam and Eve together? They were naked and not ashamed. What happened?

While they were living in dependence upon God, they saw life and one another through His eyes. They loved with His love. They always looked out for the other rather than self.

When they ate the poison fruit, their attention was drawn away from God and each other to their own flawed selves. They looked 'inwardly,' not 'outwardly.'

In God, they were as perfect as He was. When they severed their connection with Him via their independence (sin), they saw how inadequate and vile they were on their own without Him. It scared them to death. Literally. Instead of looking out for one another, they hid themselves and covered their own nakedness with fig leaves. Fallen man has been trying to cover his flawed nakedness ever since.

For the first time in their lives, they were afraid. As long as they were depending upon the Lord, they experienced His love, joy, and peace. Fear is the result when we lose the awareness of His love.

Before they ate the poison fruit, they were IN Christ. When they acted independently on their own, they were disconnected from Him.

At that very moment, they were OUT of Christ. Sin separates us from God. If you become separated from the very Source of Life, all your needs go unmet. Every single one of them.

Is there anything we have that we did not receive from God? Even the air we breathe, He provides FOR us. Just because God is gracious and continues to supply us with air and the essentials of life after we erroneously think we can be the 'source' of meeting our own needs, does not mean we are not dead.

A freshly cut branch from a tree still looks alive, but it is dead the minute it is severed from the tree. If we don't repent and return to depending upon Jesus as our Source, we will wither and die just like the branch.

God created Adam and Eve with needs before they ever ate the poison fruit. Needs are God's way of directing us to cling to, trust in, and rely upon Him to be our Source for everything. He delights in meeting our needs.

The fall twisted mankind's ability to get their needs met naturally by God as well as having a perfect relationship with each other. Pride entered the scene deceiving them into thinking, "We know how to get our own needs met. We can do it on our own. We don't need to depend on God. He really needs our help because He, alone, is not enough. We have to help Him."

Our Inheritance from Adam

It was God's Spirit that breathed life into Adam's human spirit. When God's spirit was withdrawn from Adam, his spirit died. And because we were IN Adam when he was separated from God as the Source of his life, everyone born thereafter was born with a spirit that was dead to God, too.

Because one person disobeyed God, many became sinners. But because one other Person obeyed God, many will be made righteous (Romans 5:19 NLT).

Adam and Eve could have eaten from the Tree of Life (Jesus). Had they done so, Jesus would have come INTO them, and they would have had eternal life because He IS eternal life.

Jesus alluded to His being the Tree of Life after He fed the five thousand with a few loaves of bread and fish.

Jesus said to them, "I tell you the truth, unless you eat the flesh of the Son of Man and drink His blood, you have no life in you. Whoever eats My flesh and drinks My blood has eternal life, and I will raise him up at the last day. For My flesh is real food and My blood is real drink. Whoever eats My flesh and drinks My blood remains in Me, and I in him (John 6:53-56 NIV).

It is a pity that the devil waylaid them before they ate the Tree of Life. If I had been God, I would have thrown them away and started over with someone who would obey me. But God did not throw us away. He pursued us with His love. He loved us so much that He sent His Son to pay the ultimate price to restore us. And not just to restore us, but to give us His very Life.

Points to Ponder

- God chose those who chose Him to be IN Christ before the foundation of the world and ordained that we be holy and blameless IN Him.
- God gave mankind free will to choose. God gave Adam and Eve the choice to live in dependence upon Him, or to live independently apart from Him.
- Adam and Eve were IN Christ and totally dependent upon Him to meet all their needs until they ate the poison fruit.
- Their sin disconnected them from God, and He ceased to be the Source of their life.
- Since God is the Source of Life, they died spiritually when they sinned just like God said they would.
- Spiritual death means to be cut off from God, disconnected from Him.
- Because they chose poorly, mankind was left on their own to be the source of meeting their needs, solving their own problems, and trying to live successfully.
- We inherited Adam and Eve's spiritual death and separation from God upon our physical birth.
- Had they eaten the fruit of the Tree of Life first, they would have had eternal life.
- The Tree of Life is Jesus. He IS eternal life.
- They would have been eternally ONE with Him.
- Their true nature then would have been based on their spiritual BIRTH as a child of God, not on their physical behavior.
- Jesus would have been IN them as they were IN Him.

Section Four: The Mystery Unlocked!

The Keys to the Kingdom

And that's not all. You will have complete and free access to God's kingdom, KEYS TO OPEN ANY AND EVERY DOOR: no more barriers between heaven and earth, earth and heaven. A 'yes' on earth is 'yes' in heaven. A 'no' on earth is 'no' in heaven" (Matthew 16:19 MSG, capitals mine).

"What I'm trying to do here is get you to relax, not be so preoccupied with getting so you can respond to God's giving. People who don't know God and the way He works fuss over these things, but you know both God and how He works. Steep yourself in God-reality, God-initiative, God-provisions. You'll find all your everyday human concerns will be met. Don't be afraid of missing out. You're My dearest friends! THE FATHER WANTS TO GIVE YOU THE VERY KINGDOM ITSELF" (Luke 12:29-32 MSG, capitals mine).

What we will learn in this section:

- God not only wants to give us the keys to the Kingdom, He wants to give us the Kingdom itself.
- The Kingdom belongs to dead people who have been resurrected by the King.
- The key verse that unlocks this mystery is found in Galatians 2:20.
- Dead people don't need help. They need life.
- As God's children, Jesus IS our life.
- Jesus could do nothing without His Father living FOR Him and THROUGH Him.
- Jesus came to model for us a truly dependent life where God lives in us, through us, for us, and as us.

Opening Thoughts

"This is the resting place, let the weary rest"; and, "This is the place of repose" - but they would not listen. So then, the word of the Lord to them will become: Do and do, do and do, rule on rule, rule on rule; a little here, a little there - so that they will go and fall backward, be injured and snared and captured (Isaiah 28:12-13 NIV).

Christ IN you is a mystery to religious people. Religion tells us to live 'a' Christian life. In other words, act like Jesus. 'Rotsa ruck' on that as Scooby Doo would say. Only one person ever lived like Jesus and that is Jesus, Himself. He lived THE Christian life.

Religion says that Christianity is something we DO. It is all about works. Striving to attain perfection by our performance, behavior, and obedience to the rules. Religion is based on appearances, wearing masks so that no one knows how rotten we really are. According to religion, our identity is based on 'doing.'

Jesus tells us to relax and rest in Him. He will live for us, through us, in us, and as us. All we have to 'do' is trust Him, get out of His way, and let Him live His life IN us. Our identity is based on our spiritual 'birth,' not our physical behavior. On 'being,' not 'doing.'

But to as many as did receive and welcome Him, He gave the authority (power, privilege, right) TO BECOME THE CHILDREN OF GOD, that is, to THOSE WHO BELIEVE IN (ADHERE TO, TRUST IN, AND RELY ON) HIS NAME (John 1:12 AMP, capitals mine).

We became children of God by FAITH, not performance, works, or behavior. We don't earn our way into it by working for it. As children, we are born into God's family.

For it is by grace you have been saved, through faith — and this not from yourselves, it is the gift of God— NOT BY

WORKS, so that no one can boast (Ephesians 2:8-10 NIV, capitals mine).

Religious people are tired, worn out, and burned out trying to do what only Jesus can do. Remember the WWJD wrist bands? What Would Jesus Do? We might know what Jesus would do, but we certainly cannot 'do' what Jesus would 'do.' Only He can do what He does.

I was religious for years. A Pharisee of Pharisees. I was going to 'do' something great for Jesus. After all, He died for me. The least I could do was to live for Him. I never realized that dead people cannot live for anyone. By His grace, I am now a 'recovering' Pharisee.

One day, God had mercy on me. He completely transformed my old religious belief system.

Our belief system is what we believe about:

- God
- Ourselves
- Others
- Life in general.

We developed our belief system by:

- What we have been TAUGHT.
- What we have OBSERVED.
- What we have PERSONALLY LEARNED.
- Our LIFE EXPERIENCES.

Our belief system is the most important thing about us. It will determine the quality of the life we live, and the choices we make. It will determine whether we live eternally and abundantly IN Christ, or exist in eternal death, separated from the life of Jesus.

Remember what A.W. Tozer said: "What comes to your mind when you think about God is the most important thing about you."

This book has been the most difficult thing the Lord has ever asked me to do. We (Jesus and me) have been writing this book on and off for over two years. The devil knows that Tozer is right. he has resisted, obstructed, harassed, and distracted us at every turn. he knows that the truth contained in these pages will transform your life and set you free from the bondage of religion, sin, and self.

The truths revealed in this book literally transformed my life. I'm talking about right now, not when I die and go to heaven. It will do the same for you. I guarantee it. All you have to 'do' is stop trying to live 'a' Christian life, and simply trust Jesus to live 'the' Christian life FOR you. What have you got to lose?

Religion told me I would 'experience' these truths after I died. I did die to self, and Jesus became my life as you will see in the pages that follow. But I know you want to 'see' some evidence right now. Okay.

Growing up, I was deathly afraid of rejection. I did not know, much less believe, that God loved and accepted me unconditionally. I needed acceptance, so I tried to get it from people. I found that if I pleased people and did what they wanted me to do, then most would accept me. Problem was, I could not please them all, and ultimately, they ended up rejecting me in spite of all I could do to please them. I lived in constant fear and anxiety.

When we moved from our hometown to attend seminary and pastor a church, I was a nervous wreck. I had to take four Benadryl every night to keep from scratching myself to death. I never slept. My heart rate was over ninety bpm lying in the bed. I was a heart attack waiting to happen.

65

I was so performance driven. I had to make straight A's, had to have the biggest and best church, never make a mistake, start out perfect and get better every day.

I lived that way for years until God intervened and met me so miraculously on July 22, 2007. (To find out what happened then, read our next book, *My Past is HIStory*.)

I still had trouble sleeping after my awakening. That's an oxymoron, isn't it? Somebody gave me an Ambien about ten years ago, and I slept all night for the first time ever. I have been taking it ever since. It shuts down the constant stream of thoughts running through my mind so I can sleep. I couldn't sleep without it, or so I thought.

Not long ago, I went to the pharmacy to refill my pills. They told me that they could not refill it for seven more days because it was a controlled substance. I was completely out of pills. That was very strange since I had a three month supply, and I only took one pill a day. That didn't seem possible.

Now I preach to people all the time about letting Jesus live FOR us. That He is our life, and we don't live any longer. He lives in us, through us, for us, and as us. Jesus never worries because He trusts His Father completely. And He is my life. Therefore, I should not worry and fret either.

And there I was standing in the pharmacy about to have a panic attack over not being able to sleep for a week. Then I heard Him say:

"Kenny, you don't need the pills any more. You never did need them. I sleep just fine. You and I are ONE. What I do, you do, and what you do, I do. As a matter of fact, I slept soundly on the deck of a boat in the middle of a raging storm. I AM your life now. I will be sleeping tonight. You can sleep IN Me if you want to. Or you can try to go to sleep on your own. How's that working for you? Do you trust Me, or not?"

I believed Him. At that very moment, my anxiety melted away like a snowball in the desert. That night when I went to bed, I told Jesus: "Lord, I'm sleeping IN You and WITH You tonight. Thanks for shutting my mind down so we can sleep."

I rolled over and slept like a rock. The next night, the devil said to me: "Last night was a fluke. You are going to be up all night tonight."

I simply said, "Good night, Jesus. See you in the morning." And I slept even better than the night before. I have slept soundly and pill-less ever since.

Remember I told you that Jesus living IN you is simple, but not easy. It is not easy because the world, the flesh, and the devil will never stop hounding you to take control. To fix everything yourself on your own. But that's okay. You simply depend on Jesus even more. You relax IN Him.

The devil prompts you to try harder in your own strength and wisdom when victory lies in our surrender to Christ's control. He has already won the victory over the world, the flesh, and the devil. All we have to do is stand firm and keep believing.

I HAVE BEEN CRUCIFIED WITH CHRIST and I no longer live, but Christ lives in me. (Galatians 2:20 NIV, emphasis mine).

I have come to believe that Galatians 2:20 is the key verse in all of Scripture that explains the New Covenant Life IN Christ. When you understand the meaning of this passage, and you filter all the other verses in the Bible through this verse, all the pieces of the mystery come together in a beautiful mosaic. The Bible will come alive for you as never before. It becomes a love letter, not a rule book. I can hardly wait to share it with you.

Why do we have such difficulty receiving God's grace and allowing Jesus to live His life in us, through us, for us, and as us?

First, we don't really understand what the Lord Jesus did on the cross. Next, we do not understand what happened to us on the cross. We know that Jesus died on the cross for our sins, but not many of us understand that we died, too.

Since we are confused about what Jesus accomplished on the cross, many of us are trying to die to self. Every man-made religion teaches self-denial and dying to self but Scripture simply says, "You died! Your old man is dead already."

What do we think happened when we were baptized? We were re-enacting our co-crucifixion with Christ:

Or do you not know that as many of us as were baptized into Christ Jesus were baptized into His death? (Romans 6:3).

Many of us say, "But I'm still a mess. I'm still battling with sin." That may be so, but we will gain nothing by trying to do what God has already done. The work of the cross is finished. Take a look at what Watchman Nee said in *The Normal Christian Life*:

"Let me tell you, YOU HAVE DIED! You are done with! You are ruled out! The self you loathe is on the Cross IN Christ. And **"he that is dead is freed from sin"** (Romans 6:7). This is the Gospel for Christians. Our crucifixion can never be made effective by will or by effort, but only by accepting what the Lord Jesus has already done on the Cross."

We did not die the first time we responded to God's grace, and we did not die when we were baptized. We died 2000 years ago, long before we were born! Now this sounds mysterious to those who are perishing, but to those of us who are being saved it is the power of God (1 Corinthians 1:18).

Here's another quote from Watchman Nee:

"Must we ask God to crucify us? Never! When Christ was crucified we were crucified; and his crucifixion is past; therefore, ours cannot be future... That we have died in Christ is not merely a doctrinal position, it is an eternal and indisputable fact."

Our birth determines our destination. If we think we are still in Adam, then the best we can hope for is to be a decent sinner. But when we believe that we died with Christ, we will be empowered to live with Him in the here and now (2 Tim 2:11).

God is not only the Lord of our present and future, He is also the Lord of our past. When we were born again, He gave us a brand new life complete with a brand new past. Now that's great news! We have a completely new history! And it all begins at the cross.

When Paul said, **"I have been crucified with Christ and I no longer live, but Christ lives in me"** (Galatians 2:20), he was celebrating his co-baptism and resurrection with Jesus. Paul understood there is no real life outside of Christ and those who seek to live independently on the basis of their own understanding and resources ultimately lose their true selves. But when we depend totally on Him, then we discover who we really are, and we begin to really live.

What happened to us at the cross? The short answer is, "WE DIED!" This is one of the most significant things that ever happened to us; however, it is a shame that so many of us don't know or understand it! It would be wonderful if we could give a testimony about our past like this:

"I was born, I did some stuff, then I died. I was crucified with Christ and that old self no longer lives." That's basically what Paul was saying in Galatians chapter two. He also said that the basis of our new life with Him is supposed to be a revelation that we died with Him:

This is a faithful saying: For if we died with Him, We shall also live with Him (2 Timothy 2:11).

In order to receive His resurrected life, we have to die first. No death. No resurrection. Know death. Know resurrection.

We know what happened to Jesus on the cross, but not everyone knows what happened to us. Therefore many are striving to become someone they already are, and they're fighting for something they already have. They see themselves as servants instead of sons and daughters of Almighty God.

When we were born again, God did an amazing work in our life. He gave us a glorious new past and a completely new life. He changed everything there is to change about us. One thing God left unchanged was our mind, our way of thinking. Only we can change that as we surrender to the revelation knowledge of the Holy Spirit.

In order to experience the victorious life that God wants us to live, we need to change the way we think, **"and be renewed in the spirit of your mind"** (Ephesians 4:23).

Our thought patterns are shaped by our past. So which past do we identify with? Our 'old self' history or our 'new self' history? If we want to see a paradigm shift in our life, we must look to Jesus, look to the cross, and change the way we think:

Do not be conformed to this world, but be transformed by the renewing of your mind... (Romans 12:2a).

Abraham, Levi, and Melchizedek

Christ died on the cross two thousand years ago. I'm only #?&! years old. How could I have been crucified with Him?

Allow me to illustrate with a story from the Bible.

Abraham, the Father of our Faith, had a nephew named Lot who lived in Sodom. The King of Sodom belonged to a coalition of five kings who went to war against another coalition of four kings. Sodom was defeated and all the people of Sodom were taken into captivity along with the spoils of war. When Abraham learned that Lot and his family had been kidnapped, he sprang into action to get him back.

Abraham took 318 men of his household and whipped up on the kings who took Lot and his family. He rescued them and collected all the spoils.

About that time, a great High Priest of God named Melchizedek came out of the nowhere and blessed Abraham. No one has ever seen this Priest before, or since. Many believe him to be the pre-incarnate Christ. After Melchizedek blessed him, Abraham paid a tithe, ten percent of the spoils, to Melchizedek in honor of the Most High God (Genesis 14).

In Hebrews 7:9-10, it says that Levi paid a tithe to Melchizedek when their ancestor Abraham paid a tithe to him. For although Levi wasn't born yet, the seed from which he came was in Abraham's body when Melchizedek collected the tithe from him.

Levi was the great-grandson of Abraham. He was not even a twinkle in his great-grandpa's eye, and yet Levi was credited with paying the tithe, too. How did Levi get credit for that?

Because when Abraham paid the tithe, Levi was in his body… his loins… his bloodline. Therefore, whatever Abraham did, Levi received the same credit because He was family. It was as if Levi paid the tithes himself although he never actually paid them.

71

Okay, Kenny, where are you going with this?

I'm so glad you asked. Talk about the Good News! Take a look.

Even as [in His love] He chose us [actually picked us out for Himself as His own] IN Christ before the foundation of the world, that we should be holy (consecrated and set apart for Him) and blameless in His sight (Ephesians 1:4 AMP).

Before the foundation of the world, Father God placed us IN CHRIST… into His bloodline… into His family. That is how much He loved us. We are set apart, holy and blameless because we are IN CHRIST. WOW!!!

And because we are IN CHRIST just as Levi was IN ABRAHAM, everything Jesus did, we get credit for doing just like Levi got credit for what Abraham did.

Don't go away. It gets better.

The religious people of Jesus's day thought they were keeping the rules fairly well and were proud of it. So when Jesus preached His Sermon on the Mount, He put the hammer down on them.

So you must be perfect, just as your Father in heaven is perfect (Matthew 5:48 NCV).

That pretty much slammed the door on any hope of being good enough to meet God's standard for acceptance and righteousness. Perfection was what God required in order to be in right standing with Him. Nobody's perfect. That's a pretty hopeless situation. But not so fast.

Look what Jesus did. He lived a perfect life for us, in us, as us, and through us. Since we are IN HIM, whatever Jesus did, we get credit for it just as if we had done it ourselves. Talk about a great deal!

The Bible tells us that **"the wages of sin is death"** (Romans 6:23). Sin demands that someone must die in order to pay for our sin debt.

Question: Where were you and I when Jesus died on the cross? You got it. We were IN Him.

I was put to death on the cross with Christ, and I do not live anymore... (Galatians 2:20 NCV).

We died with Him on the cross, and we got a receipt for our sin debt. Paid in full! Jesus died for us and as us. And we got credit for paying our sin debt just as if we died ourselves.

For He raised us from the dead along with Christ and seated us with Him in the heavenly realms because we are united with Christ Jesus (Ephesians 2:6-7 NLT).

When Jesus rose from the dead, where were we? IN HIM. We were raised with Him because we were IN HIM. United with Him. One with Him. Fused with Him. Wherever He goes, we go. Wherever we go, He goes.

We were raised to life just as He was. And now we are seated with Him in heaven. It is going to astound us when we get to heaven and realize that we have been there the whole time!

Now let me ask you something. Did we live a perfect life as God required? Did we die on the cross to pay for our sins? Did we rise from the dead?

Yes! Yes! Yes!

We did because we are united with Jesus... ONE with Him. Fused with Him. As He is, so are we in this world (1 John 4:17). We are in His loins... in His bloodline... in His family... in His lineage. And whatever Jesus did, we get credit for it just as if we had done it ourselves.

And that's not so hard to believe if you can grasp the truth of Galatians 2:20.

How much work did we do to accomplish this great miracle? None! Jesus did it all FOR us.

When He accomplished this great feat of grace, He cried from the cross, "IT IS FINISHED!" There is nothing left for us to do but to glorify Him and enjoy Him forever. Amen!

The 'Old Me' Does Not Live Anymore

I was put to death on the cross with Christ, and I DO NOT LIVE ANYMORE — it is Christ who lives IN me (Galatians 2:20 NCV, capitals mine).

What do you mean, the 'old me' does not live anymore?

Okay, when Adam and Eve ate the poison fruit, they became disconnected from God. God is the source of life. Whenever we become disconnected from life, we call that DEAD.

After the fall, their human spirit was so corrupted, it could not be fixed. It was dead to God. It had to go. That is why we were crucified with Christ on the cross. The 'old self' had to be put to death.

The wages of sin is death. If you sin, act on your own rather than depend on the Lord, you will die. That means you are separated from God as the Source of Life for eternity. The way we stay alive is to remain totally dependent and connected to Him by faith for life and everything else. That is the way He wants it.

Someone had to pay our sin debt for us, or else we would have been lost forever. Jesus died on the cross to pay our debt.

Three things happened on the cross:

- Jesus died to pay for the wages of our sin.
- Our old self, which could not be fixed, died with Him.
- We were freed from sin because sin has no effect on dead people.

Your 'old self' died and that 'old you' does not live anymore. That 'old you' wanted to live independently without depending upon God. That 'old you' was held captive by sin and the devil. You had to be set free, and the only way you could be free was for the 'old you' to die.

But you say, "I'm still living. I'm still walking around doing stuff. How can I be dead?"

The Headless Turtle

Two friends were walking along a river one day when they spied a turtle whose head had been chopped off. But strangely, the turtle was still walking along the bank.

One said, "How can that turtle be walking when his head has been chopped off? You are dead without a head."

The other said, "He can't be dead because he is still walking."

About that time a friend came along, and they asked him, "See that turtle. His head is chopped off, and he is still walking. Is he dead, or alive?"

The friend replied, "Oh, he is dead alright. He just doesn't know it."

The apostle Paul addressed this same issue with the Romans.

For we know that our old self was crucified with Him so that the body of sin might be done away with, that we should no longer be slaves to sin— because anyone who has died has been freed from sin... In the same way, COUNT YOURSELVES DEAD TO SIN but alive to God in Christ Jesus (Romans 6:6-7, 11 NIV capitals mine).

We have to reckon ourselves dead by faith because God says we are dead. Our soul may not feel like we are dead, but we are dead because God says we are. Are we going to base our life on fact, or on feelings?

Don't Know Up From Down?

Amy Svoboda knew better. She was a fighter pilot par excellent. She was chief of training for the 355th Wing's 354th Fighter Squadron at Davis-Monthan AFB. She was a 1989 graduate of the Air Force Academy and the second female fighter pilot in the 355th Wing to die. All the years of training. The intensive study. The discipline. All neglected for just a matter of seconds, but that's all it took.

Capt. Svoboda was flying a routine training mission over the Arizona desert near Tucson. She dropped her four bombs and twisted her plane at a steep angle to view the impact. She was warned to check her dive angle but failed to do so. Because she failed to consult her instruments, Capt. Svoboda continued to fly upside-down while thinking all the time she was right-side up. She also felt that she was climbing when, indeed, she was diving.

Force Base said, "I am certain that Amy thought she was right-side up, because we found the engines at almost full power."

A number of factors figured into the crash. The darkness. Impaired vision from the glare of the bombs. The 'routineness' of the mission. Negligence. Misplaced trust in feelings. Capt. Amy Svoboda should not be dead today. She knew better. Even though her occupation was hazardous, she had all the technological advantages at her disposal to keep her safe. She was only negligent for about 4 or 5 seconds, and her plane hit the ground nose first at over 400 miles per hour!

As God's children, we are not unlike Capt. Svoboda. We, too, know better. We have been highly trained. We have studied to show ourselves approved unto God (2 Timothy 2:15). The Holy Spirit has written the Word upon our hearts. We have been given wings with which to mount up as eagles (Isaiah 40:31). Wings called 'trust' and 'obey.' However, our trust is only as good as the object in which we are trusting, and that object must be reliable.

For Amy, it was her training and her instruments. For us, it is the Word of God. It is much more reliable than any instrument panel in even the most sophisticated jet fighter. We must trust it and act upon it, or else we will crash and burn as well.

When Capt. Svoboda needed her object of trust the most, when she was in darkness and her vision was impaired, she failed to rely upon the one thing that could have saved her life... the truth of her instrument panel. Beloved, we must not make the same mistake.

Are you in a dark place in your life right now? Are you seeing God's plan for your life clearly at this moment? If your life is spinning out of control, you must check your instruments, the Word of God. God's ways are not our ways. Without God's guidance system, we can be flying upside-down and think we are right-side up. We can think we are climbing when in reality we are in a nose-dive.

Let's do a quick flight check: Are you confused about some things going on in your life right now? Has the glare of the world dimmed your spiritual vision? Has your walk (or flight) with God become routine and hum-drum? Are you neglecting the Word of God (your instrument panel) and prayer (your communication with the tower)? Have you logged your flight plan with the tower and received the Commander's approval? Are you walking by faith, or by your feelings?

Every pilot goes through a thorough checklist before every mission. We need to do a daily check-up to make sure we are not taking our flight with the Lord for granted. You may have checked every item on your pre-flight checklist. I'm sure Capt. Svoboda did as well. However, there is one other essential necessary to ensure a successful mission: obey what God is telling you, not what you feel He is saying to you.

You can have the finest and most accurate instrument panel in the world, but you must obey what it tells you to do. Instruments don't lie. Neither does God's Word. We cannot always trust what we feel. Feelings will often lie to us. They are called, 'lying' emotions. Amy's lied to her, and now she's lying six feet under.

Fellow warrior, the warfare is intensifying. We are not in a training mission. We are in live combat. All-out war! We are in a life and death struggle with the enemy for the souls of men and women, boys and girls not the least of which is our own. We cannot afford to be derelict in our duties. We must be unconditionally faithful to our Commander-In-Chief, the Lord Jesus.

Capt. Svoboda failed to trust and obey for 4 seconds. 4 measly seconds. Not long at all, but long enough to usher her into eternity. She was warned and trained. So are we.

"Be self-controlled and alert. Your enemy the devil prowls around like a roaring lion looking for someone to devour" (I Peter 5:8)

"Be always on the watch, and pray that you may be able to escape all that is about to happen" (Luke 21:36).

There comes a time when knowing what to do must be translated into doing what we know. Amy knew better. Let's make sure we do, too.

The Law of Gravity vs. the Law of Aerodynamic

I want you to notice something here. The Lord washed away all our 'sins' on the cross; however, His death did not get rid of the power of sin. SIN, the noun, not the verb, still exists. Let me explain.

SIN (independence) is like the law of gravity. It pulls on us 24/7. The Bible calls it the law of sin and death. In Romans chapter 8, Paul says that the law of the Spirit of Life in Christ has set us free from the law of sin and death.

Jesus defeated sin and death on the cross. He overcame them. IN Him, we are overcomers, too, because He is our life. When we trust Him to live His life in us, through us, for us, and as us, we triumph over the law of sin and death.

An airplane is able to fly because of the law of aerodynamics. The curvature of the wings are shaped in such a way that the rushing air over the top of the wings creates lift underneath. The law of aerodynamics is greater than the law of gravity.

Mind you, gravity does not cease to exist so that the plane can fly. The law of aerodynamics supercedes the law of gravity. As long as the wings remain intact and the plane has a means of propulsion, it will fly. Gravity is still in effect, but the law of aerodynamic overcomes it.

From a spiritual standpoint, IN Christ we have two wings, too. One is called TRUST. The other is called OBEY. When Jesus is the Source of our 'propulsion,' and we keep our wings intact, sin is ineffective in our lives just as gravity is ineffective with the airplane.

The airplane and our walk IN Christ both require two wings. TRUST alone is not enough if we don't act on what we say we believe. Acting (obeying) alone will not work if our obedience is not based on the truth of God. It takes both wings to overcome gravity and sin.

As the old song says, "Trust and obey. For there's no other way. To be happy in Jesus, but to trust and obey.

Gun vs. Bullets

Let's take another example. Let's say that sin is the bullet, and the 'old self' is the gun. There are still bullets, but the gun (our 'old self') died with Him on the cross. The bullets are harmless without a gun with which to shoot them

Dead People Don't Sin

Our old corrupted spirit was dead in sin (Ephesians 2:1). When our 'old self' was crucified on the cross with Jesus, our 'old self' died. Dead people don't sin. They can't even be tempted to sin. We have been set free from the power of sin.

Our old sin corrupted spirit is dead, gone, annihilated, and erased forever. But if you don't believe the 'old you' is dead, you will not allow Jesus to live FOR you. You will keep trying to live for yourself, even though your 'old self' is dead. Remember the turtle?

Faith is an action word. You have to act on what you say you believe, or you will not experience the truth. That is why Paul says: **"COUNT YOURSELVES DEAD TO SIN but alive to God in Christ Jesus."**

Many children of God are like the turtle. They are dead. They just don't know it.

Religion told me to try as hard as I could to be good and act like Jesus. But how can I be good and act like Jesus if I am dead? How can you help a dead person? Dead people don't need help. They need life.

The 'old me' is really dead. I am no longer the source of the 'living, producing, doing, and fixing' in my life. God fused Himself with me. He is the Source of my life now. The entirety of my existence now depends upon my 'oneness with Christ.' Jesus turned my life right side up and my ME into WE.

I relax into this reality and receive it like a child. Death brought me forgiveness. Resurrection brought me righteousness. Death took away my sins. Resurrection infused the life of Christ inside of me. I needed both the death and the resurrection. God gave me a brand new human spirit to replace my old corrupted spirit.

And I will give you a new heart, and I will put a new spirit in you. I will take out your stony, stubborn heart and give you a tender, responsive heart. And I will put my Spirit in you so that you will follow my decrees and be careful to obey my regulations (Ezekiel 36:26-27 NLT).

Notice the four 'I wills' in this passage. God does all this FOR us. He takes out the heart of our 'old self' that was so self-centered and gave us His heart and His Spirit. Jesus' heart now beats in our 'new self.' Jesus delights in the Father's will. And now, we also delight in doing His will because Jesus is our life. It comes natural for Him and should come natural for us if we only trust Him.

At the resurrection, Jesus raised me from the dead in Him. Right there I put on the Lord Jesus Christ. Right there I was born again. Right there I was given eternal life. Right there I died and was buried. Right there I became a new creation. Right there all old things passed away, Right there all things became new. Right there it was no longer I who lives but Christ lives IN me. It all happened instantaneously.

This all happened at the resurrection, and it became literal and real the moment Christ became my life. It is not something that will happen in the future. I am not a dirty creature trying to clean up. I am a new creation with Christ's perfect life living in me right now.

Therefore, if anyone is in Christ, he is a new creation; old things have passed away; behold, all things have become new (2 Corinthians 5:17 NKJV).

The Two Sides of the Cross

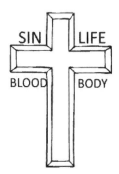

There are only two kinds of people in the world. Dead people and alive people. You are either dead in sin, or alive in Jesus. There is no middle ground. There are no good Christians, or bad Christians. Good Christians are perfect in Christ. There is no such thing as a bad Christian because our identity is based on our spiritual birth, not our physical behavior.

God has given us eternal life, and this life is in His Son. He who has the Son has life; he who does not have the Son of God does not have life (1 John 5:11-12 NIV).

Religion only told me about one side of the cross... the 'sin' side. If you ask a religious person why Jesus came to earth, the majority will tell you He came to die for our sins.

What can wash away our sins? Nothing but the blood of Jesus. And that is absolutely true. But there is a lot more to the cross than just forgiveness of our sins.

There is a SIN side of the cross, and there is a LIFE side. Sin kills us by separating us from God who is the Source of all Life. The 'old self' that was bound by sin had to die. Sin has no power over dead people. That is why we were crucified with Jesus.

Yes, the blood washes away our sins, but the blood also gives us life. The book of Leviticus tells us that life is in the blood.

Blood Test

Let's say you get sick and go the doctor. The first thing the doctor usually does is check your blood. The doctor can tell why you are sick by what is in your blood. If your blood is good, you are healthy. If there is stuff in your blood that's not supposed to be there, then you are sick.

Jesus blood on the 'sin' side of the cross accomplishes two things:

- It washes away our sins.
- It gives us His life. Remember, life is in the blood.

On the 'life' side of the cross, Jesus' body died because He became sin FOR us. His death paid for the wages for our sin. He gave His life FOR us.

Christ had no sin, but GOD MADE HIM TO BECOME SIN for us so that in Christ we could become right with God (2 Corinthians 5:21 NCV, capitals mine).

The Cross Is Curative, not Punitive

Father God did not punish Jesus for our sins. Jesus BECAME sin FOR us. Papa poured His wrath out on the sin Jesus became for us, not Jesus, Himself.

Think about this. Every sin that has ever been committed. Every sin that ever will be committed, Jesus took upon Himself. Hitler's sin. Every serial killer's sin. Every rapist's sin. Osama Bin Laden's sin. Your sin. My sin. Everyone's sin. Past, present, and future sin. Jesus held all that sin in place while Papa nuked it with His wrath.

Jesus paid our sin debt with His Life. Then He was buried. On the third day, Jesus rose from the grave never to die again. He cured our terminal sin disease on the cross once and for all time.

Where were we when Jesus died? IN Him. Where were we when Jesus rose again from the dead? IN Him. Everything Jesus did on the cross FOR us, we get credit for because we were IN Him when He did it.

Our 'old self' with its corrupted spirit died on the cross with Jesus. Our 'new self' came out of the grave with Jesus. It is Jesus who now lives in us, through us, for us, and as us.

Religion has robbed us by not telling us about the 'life' side of the cross. Religion has told us that we still live, but we don't. Religion has told us we just need a little help from Jesus to live a good life. Dead people cannot live good lives. Dead people don't even live bad lives. Dead people don't even live. Period.

Let's illustrate the necessity of understanding both sides of the cross.

Suppose you have a corpse who died of a terminal disease lying on a gurney in front of you. You have the power to give one of two things to the corpse, but not both. You can heal the corpse's disease, or you can raise him from the dead.

If you choose to heal him, then you have a healthy corpse; however, he is still dead as a hammer.

If you choose to raise him from the dead, he is alive, but he still has the terminal disease. He is going to die again.

Christ did both FOR us on the cross. He healed our terminal sin disease, and He raised us from the dead. Now He didn't just give us life, He gave us HIS LIFE! Eternal life.

Christ Lives IN Me!

I was put to death on the cross with Christ, and I do not live anymore — IT IS CHRIST WHO LIVES IN ME (Galatians 2:20 NCV, capitals mine).

Points to Ponder

- We were chosen in Christ before the foundation of the world.
- Since we were IN Him, everything He did, we got credit for even though we did not actually do it ourselves.
- Our 'old sinful human spirit' died with Him on the cross. Our 'old self' was removed, eradicated, and annihilated forever.
- Forgiving our sins, removing our old, stony heart, and giving us a new heart is great, but God's ultimate goal is for us to be fused, joined, and united together as ONE with Him.
- Our death sentence for our sins was paid for when He died.
- All our sins--- past, present, and future--- are forgiven, forgotten, forever.
- All these things are true, but they will not become effectual for us if we do not believe (cling to, trust in, rely upon, put your whole weight upon) they are true and act upon them.
- We are now dead to sin, but alive to God through Christ Jesus, our Lord.
- We live now because He lives. He is our life.

Section Five: The Mystery Illustrated

Preface: Common Roadblocks to 'Getting It'

In this section, I want to share with you some common hang-ups people have about Jesus living in us, through us, for us, and as us. This life IN Christ is so simple. The only thing hard about it is our soul and flesh's reluctance to give up control of our lives. That is ironic since we have no life apart from Him.

The mind is the doorway into this new life IN Christ. We will never live beyond what we believe. Religion has badly damaged the old operating system of our mind. Religion has falsely programmed us to believe that the Christian life is about doing things FOR God. That our right standing with Him is based on our behavior. That kind of brainwashing is very difficult to overcome.

Intellectual understanding will never be able to comprehend our life IN Christ. It makes no sense. How can the God of the universe be bigger than the universe and still fit inside of me? As Mr. Spock would say, "That is illogical."

Our minds have to be renewed by the revelation of the Holy Spirit. For example, have you ever read a verse a thousand times and then one day you read it and you totally understand what it means? It is like reading it for the very first time. That is revelation knowledge.

From Heart to Head

I have heard people say that what's in their head needs to drop down into their heart. That is not true. Jesus took out our old stony heart and gave us a new heart. His heart. He took out our old corrupted human spirit and gave us a new spirit which He fused with His Spirit making us ONE with Him.

We know the truth in our HEART. What the heart knows and understands needs to 'jump up' into our minds, not fall from our mind to our heart. This truth is so wonderful, it is difficult to wrap our minds around it.

The heart is the junction of our body, soul, and spirit. It is where your belief system lives. It is the most important thing about you as A.W. Tozer says. That is why the Bible tells us to **"guard your heart with all diligence, for out of it flows the issues of life"** (Proverbs 4:23).

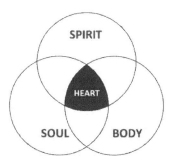

The heart is being fed information from the body, soul, and spirit. Your true identity IN Christ is found in your SPIRIT which is ONE and the same with Him. That is why we walk in the Spirit so that we will not be deceived by the world, the flesh, and the devil.

The goal of this section is to help your mind grasp what the heart already knows. Jesus knew very well that the shortest distance between the truth and our heart is a story. A word picture, if you will. And He was the Master Storyteller.

My Prayer as We Begin this Section

When I think of all this, I fall to my knees and pray to the Father, the Creator of everything in heaven and on earth. I pray that from His glorious, unlimited resources He will empower you with inner strength through His Spirit. Then Christ will make His home in your hearts as you trust in Him. Your roots will grow down into God's love and keep you strong. And may you have the power to understand, as all God's people should, how wide, how long, how high, and how deep His love is. May you experience the love of Christ, though it is too great to understand fully. Then you will be made complete with all the fullness of life and power that comes from God.

Now all glory to God, who is able, through His mighty power at work within us, to accomplish infinitely more than we might ask or think (Ephesians 3:14-21 NLT).

Are you ready? Then let's get started.

Grace Is Not a License to Sin

Some people erroneously think that grace is a license to sin. They think that grace means that God does not care how we live. That He loves us anyway no matter what. And He does. But it grieves His heart to see us futilely pursuing the desires of our heart in all the wrong places.

People also falsely believe that God's love is based on our behavior. If we do good, God blesses us. If we do bad, God will punish us. That is 'performance-based acceptance.'

When Christ is our life, we have 'acceptance-based performance.' I do what I do because I love Jesus and who I am IN Him, not out of duty because I have to do it, or else.

A young girl was asked by her boyfriend to go somewhere she did not want to go. He asked her, "Are you afraid your daddy will hurt you if you go, and he finds out?"

"No, I'm afraid it will hurt my Daddy," she replied.

90

Religion's motivation is fear. God's motivation is love.

I told one lady that Jesus was her life and that she did not live anymore. I told her she was holy, righteous, unconditionally loved, and accepted because Jesus was all of that, and Jesus was her life. What was true of Jesus was true of her because she was ONE with Him.

The lady said, "Do you mean that if I go out to a bar and get drunk, commit adultery, and lie to my husband, Jesus is okay with that? He forgives me regardless? Grace means I can do whatever I want to do no matter what?"

To which I responded, "If you could do that in all good conscience with no remorse, then Jesus is not your life. Jesus hates sin. Jesus would not do that. That would be abhorrent to Him. And it would be to you if Jesus is your life."

She replied, "But I'm not Jesus."

I responded, "You are Jesus because He IS your life. Salvation is not asking God to forgive you of your sins, and then trying to live a good life. Salvation is Jesus IN you, living His life as you. He is eternal life. That is salvation. He IS your life, and the 'old you' doesn't live anymore.

If Jesus is not living His life in you, through you, for you, and as you, then you are not a Christian, saved, born again, or whatever you want to call it.

God has given us eternal life, and this life is in his Son. He who has the Son has life; he who does not have the Son of God does not have life (1 John 5:11-12 NIV).

Salvation is not something we do. Salvation is Someone we are.

Grace is not a license to do whatever we want. It is the power to do what we ought IN Christ. He is our power, our strength, our everything. And we can do what we ought because Jesus will do it FOR us if we will only allow Him to do so.

91

Can I Lose My Salvation?

When I coached high school basketball, I had a kid who gave his heart to Jesus. The Lord really transformed Him. He told everybody who would listen about Jesus. If no one listened, he would witness to the lockers.

One day he came to class and said, "Coach, I lost it!"

"What did you lose?"

"I lost my salvation!"

I snickered and replied, "Where do you think you lost it? Maybe it's in your locker, or fell out of your wallet."

"Coach, I'm serious. I thought I was saved, but I can't be."

"Why do you say that?"

"Last night my brother and I got into an argument, and I beat the daylights out of him. A Christian would never do anything like that. What am I going to do?"

"Let me ask you something, is this the first time you ever beat up your brother?"

"No."

"Before you were saved, how did it feel when you beat him up?"

"Well, I hate to say it, but it felt good."

"How did you feel about it this time?"

"Coach, I feel terrible. I never should have done it."

"I'm glad you feel that way. It verifies your salvation experience to be true. When Jesus became your life, He gave you His nature. This kind of stuff is not who you are anymore. That is why you feel bad. What you are feeling is confirmation that Jesus is your life now."

Forgiven. Forgotten. Forever.

Okay. But when we sin after Jesus becomes our life, don't we still need to confess it and ask forgiveness?

Confess it? Yes. Feel godly sorrow over it? Yes. Ask the Lord to forgive you? No.

Let me ask you something: When Jesus died on the cross, how many of your sins were in the future? ALL of them. When Jesus forgave your sins, He forgave ALL of your sins. Past. Present. Future.

Although all our sins are forgiven, they still bring consequences even after we become ONE with Him. If I forget who I am in Jesus for a second and assault someone, I will go to jail for it. In that moment, I quit depending on Jesus and acted independently apart from Him. We call that sin. Was that sin forgiven, too, when Jesus saved me? Absolutely. Will I still go to jail? Absolutely. Understand?

We still live in an unredeemed body, controlled by an unredeemed soul, in a fallen world ruled by satan.

Sin opens the door for the flesh. The mind set on the flesh is death.

Sin for the saint still causes suffering and blocks the flow of Jesus' life through us. Jesus does not leave us. How can He? We are FUSED together. Inseparable. When we take control, we just push Him off the stool for a while. We take control instead of Him. And control for us is an illusion. We have about as much control over our life as a leaf in a hurricane.

Confession is good for the soul, but the sin has already been forgiven once and for all.

Hebrews 10:14 says that **"by one sacrifice He has made perfect forever those who are being made holy."**

When you accepted Jesus as your life, your 'old self' with all its sins passed away. It doesn't even exist anymore. Our spirit is made perfect IN Him, but our soul is still learning to trust Him. It is a work in progress.

To ask for forgiveness for sin after the Lord has washed it away reveals our unbelief.

Listen to me. Don't misunderstand me on this. Just because the sin has already been forgiven, it does not mean that my heart doesn't break over it. Anyone who can sin and remain callous about it does not have Jesus living in them.

As a matter of fact, whenever I sin now, I feel more devastated about it than I ever did before I understood that Jesus had become my life. I am a new creation now. And because I am, sin hurts and grieves me even more because I know it grieves my Lord who loves me so.

Someone once told me that when he trusted Jesus as His Lord and Savior, he believed all of his 'past' sins were forgiven. He said that he was on his own after that. Now every sin he commits, he has to confess and ask Jesus to forgive Him for his 'new' sins.

If that is true, how do you interpret this passage?

First He says: "This is the covenant I will make with them after that time, says the Lord. I will put My laws in their hearts, and I will write them on their minds."

Then He adds: "THEIR SINS AND LAWLESS ACTS I WILL REMEMBER NO MORE."

And where these have been forgiven, there is no longer any sacrifice for sin (Hebrews 10:15-18 NIV, capitals mine).

Does God forget about my sins? I still remember them. Does that mean I know something God does not? No.

Does God mean that He remembers them, but He will not bring them back up and use them against us? No.

God does not remember them because our sins do not exist anymore. Past. Present. Future. All gone. All washed away. Nothing there for God to remember. It is as if they never existed. All our old stuff has passed away. We are brand new creations IN Christ.

How can that be, you say? Here is what happened when Jesus became your life.

Therefore if any person is [ingrafted] in Christ (the Messiah) he is a new creation (a new creature altogether); THE OLD [PREVIOUS MORAL AND SPIRITUAL CONDITION] HAS PASSED AWAY. Behold, the fresh and new has come! (2 Corinthians 5:17 AMP, capitals mine).

Your 'old self' with all its sins passed away. Your previous moral and spiritual condition is gone. It does not exist anymore. Your sins thrown into the sea of forgetfulness.

You are a new creation. New in nature and design. You are fused, united, and joined to Christ. One with Him forever. You, the 'old you,' does not live anymore. Christ is your life now.

Does Christ have any sin in His life? No. Then neither do you.

Does Jesus need to be forgiven? No. Then neither do you.

Whenever you sin... act independently apart from depending upon the Lord... there are still consequences. But the sin was forgiven, erased, and eradicated the day Jesus became your life.

Jesus is still your life even when you sin. He cannot separate Himself from you because you are ONE with Him. We are made perfect IN Him forever, but our soul still chooses to act independently sometimes. When we do, we lose sight of our identity IN Him and the awareness of His presence.

The consequences of our sin and its accompanying suffering drives us back to depending on Jesus for everything. God even uses our sin, which He forgave once for all time, to motivate us to come back into dependence upon Him.

As a child of God, your sins are forgiven, forgotten, forever. The reason you still feel guilty and condemned is because you just don't believe it fully... yet.

Remember: You will never live beyond what you believe. Start living as if you are totally forgiven, because you are, and you will begin to experience true freedom IN Christ.

If Jesus Loves Me, Why Did My Car Break Down?

For a long time after Jesus became our life, I erroneously believed that life would smooth out for me from then on. No more trials and tribulations. No aggravations. I believed that life was going to be rainbows, lollipops, sunshine, and everything that's wonderful since we were together. I laugh now at how naïve I was.

Just because satan lost us to Jesus, does not mean that he is going to leave us alone. Oh, no. he simply changes tactics. he harasses us, distracts us, and puts lying thoughts into our heads. Anything he can do to keep us from waking up to our true identity and destiny IN Christ.

Have you ever put money into a vending machine and lost it without getting what you wanted? Did you just walk away and say, "Oh, well. I guess I will just go hungry today. I didn't need that money anyway." Yeah, right!

No. We pound on that machine with our fists. We kick it. Bang on it. Rock it. Scream at it. We want our food!

The devil is the same way. he is used to pushing your button to get you all upset and get your attention off Jesus. When you trust Jesus to handle satan FOR you, he gets really upset. He starts banging on you. Kicking you. Yelling lies at you. That is his modus operandi. he wants you to fight him rather than trusting in Jesus' victory over him.

Some people think that we don't need common sense after Jesus becomes our life. They think Jesus lives and moves in us supernaturally and miraculously. And the Lord does that sometimes, but mostly he communicates with us through the realm of the real world.

The more you allow Jesus to live His life in you, through you, for you, and as you, the more of a threat you and Jesus become to satan. he goes crazy trying to get you to act independently without relying upon Jesus. If he can get you disconnected from Jesus, he knows he can easily defeat you. He tried to do the same thing with Jesus. Do you think he is going to cut you some slack? Absolutely not!

Take a football game for example. There are eleven players on defense who are trying to stop one player on offense. Which player on offense are they trying to stop?

You guessed it. The one carrying the ball. They are not trying to knock down everybody else, just the one with the ball.

When the one carrying the ball is 99 yards away from a touchdown, the defense will give him a couple of yards. But if the ball carrier is only one yard away from a touchdown, the defense will claw, bite, scratch, call you dirty names, and try to pull the football out of his hands. Why? Because the ball carrier is close to scoring and helping his team defeat them.

The more of a threat you become because you are giving more and more control to Jesus (the football, if you will), the harder the devil will fight you to dislodge the ball (Jesus) from you. It is just logical. It is what it is.

Spoiler alert! We already won the game IN Jesus. So go out and play in reckless abandon. Don't get discouraged. It may look as if we are behind right now on the scoreboard, but as Yogi Berra said, "It ain't over till it's over."

What Is 'Unconditional Love?'

Love, by definition, is unconditional. Conditional love is an oxymoron. I will love you IF… is not love at all.

Love is all about freedom. It is for freedom that Christ has set us free (Galatians 5:1).

You can go anywhere in the world you want to go as long as you don't leave town. Is that true freedom? Is that real love?

God's love always gives us the power to choose. Without the power to choose, love cannot be true love. There is no freedom without choice. That is why the tree of the knowledge of good and evil was in the Garden of Eden.

You cannot make anyone love you. It is the freedom of choice that validates love. Giving others the freedom to be who they are, and to choose what they do, and where they go is the ultimate expression of love.

There is an old story [probably apocryphal, according to one Lincoln historian] that Abraham Lincoln went down to the slave block to buy a slave girl. As she looked at the white man bidding on her, she figured he was another white man going to buy her and then abuse her. He won the bid, and as he was walking away with his property, he said, "Young lady, you are free."

She said, "What does that mean?"

"It means you are free."

"Does that mean," she said, "that I can say whatever I want to say?"

Lincoln said, "Yes, my dear, you can say whatever you want to say."

"Does that mean," she said, "that I can be whatever I want to be?"

Lincoln said, "Yes, you can be whatever you want to be."

"Does that mean I can go wherever I want to go?"

He said, "Yes, you can go wherever you want to go."

The girl, with tears streaming down her face, said, "Then I will go with you."

Love vs. Fear

There are really only two forces in the universe: Love and fear. One or the other is going to control our lives.

God is all about LOVE and FREEDOM. The devil is all about FEAR and CONTROL.

Let's go back to the Garden. Adam and Eve lived free in the Garden with God who walked with them every day in the cool of the evening. All they knew was freedom and love.

They were free to eat from any tree in the Garden, including the one with the poison fruit. They were free to eat it, but they were not free from the consequences... death.

After they ate the poison fruit, they experienced fear for the first time in their lives. They ran away from God because they were afraid of Him. They believed the lie of the devil that God was not good. That he did not care about them. That they should look out for themselves and forget about that old egotistical God.

Fear tries to control everything so as to protect 'self.' My 'old self' believed that if I could control everything and everybody, then no one could harm me. But as we have previously stated, control is an illusion. We can't control ourselves, much less anybody else.

We Were Created with Needs

For a long time, I believed that man became 'needy' only after the fall. That he had no needs before he ate the poison fruit and died spiritually. I was wrong about that.

God created us with needs. Here are just a few:

Eight Common Emotional Needs

ACCEPTANCE-deliberate and ready reception with a favorable positive response. (Romans 15:7).

AFFECTION-- communicating care and closeness through physical touch and loving words. (Romans 16:16).

APPRECIATION(Praise)-communicating personal gratefulness with words and feelings. (I Corinthians 11:2).

APPROVAL-- expressed commendation; thinking and speaking well of. (Romans 14:18).

ATTENTION (Care)-- taking thought of another and conveying appropriate interest and support; entering into another's 'world.' (Acts 27:3).

ENCOURAGEMENT-- urging forward and positively persuading toward a goal. (I Thessalonians 5:11; Hebrews 10:24).

LOVE (unconditional)-- the freedom to be who I am without fear of condemnation or rejection. (Jeremiah 31:3; John 15:9).

RESPECT (Honor)-- valuing and regarding highly; conveying great worth. (Romans 12:10).

SECURITY (Peace)-- confidence of harmony in relationships; freedom from harm. (2 Thessalonians 3:16).

Why do you think God created us 'needy?'

Think about it. What is God's will for every single person on the planet?

- To live in total, absolute dependence upon Him for our every need.
- To live in intimate relationship with Him and enjoy Him forever.

God, and God alone, is the only One who can meet those needs in our lives. He is infinite and has an endless supply for every need we could ever have. He delights in meeting our needs FOR us. He never intended for us to meet our own needs.

When we were dead in our trespasses and sins, He sent His own Son to die in our place and give us His own life to live in us, through us, for us, and as us. If God gave us His best, do you think He is not going to give us the rest?

He who did not spare His own Son, but gave Him up for us all — how will He not also, along with Him, graciously give us all things? (Romans 8:32 NIV).

If everything we will ever need in our life has been provided for us if we will only trust the Lord and simply 'receive' it, then what's the problem? Why do we still live 'needy' lives? Why do we live in spiritual poverty when God has given us the keys of the Kingdom, and the very Kingdom itself?

The answer is simple: We don't trust God.

Adam and Eve trusted God before the fall, and God provided for all their needs. When they believed the lie of the devil that God was not trustworthy, they ceased going to God for the supply for all their needs.

After the fall, they were still 'needy.' Big time 'needy.' However, they cut themselves off from the Source of provision for all their needs... God, Himself.

God would have still provided for them had they come to Him and asked Him, but they did not trust Him anymore. So the only 'source' they had was themselves. They needed someone else other than God to meet their needs be that themselves, or others. As we all know, that is a dead-end road.

How Can God Love Me Unconditionally?

Love is freedom. Love makes no demands. Love has no needs. Love has no conditions. Love is 'other-focused.' Love is patient. Love is kind. Love keeps no record of wrongs. Love always protects. Love always trusts. Love always hopes. Love always perseveres (1 Corinthians 13).

God is all those things. If He is your life, and you don't live anymore, then you are all those things, too. Then why are you not experiencing it?

It God wants to be all that FOR you, and He has promised to give it to you if you simply ask, why won't you go get it? You, too, have believed the lie of the devil. You don't trust God either. Plain and simple. You are still the 'source' of meeting your needs.

God loves me unconditionally because He does not need anything from me. He doesn't need me to do anything thing for Him. He doesn't need me to love Him. He doesn't need me to act like a Christian so I don't give Him a bad name. He doesn't need me to win the world to Jesus. He could do all that without me.

God has no needs outside Himself. That is why He is ONE God who exists in THREE PERSONS... Father, Son, and Holy Spirit. Love cannot exist alone. God is love. Love must have an object upon which to bestow itself.

All of God's relational needs are met within Himself. Papa, Jesus, and the Holy Spirit all love one another and are loved by one another. God needs nothing from His creation. He is the only Self-sufficient One in the universe.

God does not DO love. He IS love. Water does not DO wet. Water IS wet by its very nature. Water never distinguishes between who deserves to be wet and who does not. If you are in the water, you are wet. If you are IN Christ, you are loved.

He cannot help Himself. He loves us for nothing. He needs nothing from us in order for Him to love us. He so enjoys loving that He wants to invite us into His family to enjoy the same love relationship He enjoys within Himself.

He loves us unconditionally because He doesn't need us. Since He needs nothing from us, He can give us freedom to be and do as we please. Love accepts us just as we are, and where we are on our journey through life. Love gives us freedom to make mistakes and even sin without ever diminishing His love for us.

God loves us unconditionally because He doesn't need anything from us. That is why it is impossible to love someone from whom you need something. You cannot give them freedom for fear they might not give you what YOU need.

We Love Because He First Loved Us

I spent the majority of my life trying to love people. After all, Jesus told us to love God with all our heart, mind, soul, and strength, and to love our neighbor as we love ourselves (Matthew 22:37-40). But I had a problem. God is love. I am not, or so I thought back then. I cannot not give what I have not first received.

I thought I was unworthy of His love because I was not doing enough for Him. I was not perfect. I was the source of my love, not the Lord. And I was empty.

When God flipped my filter and opened my eyes, these are the verses He used.

This is love: not that we loved God, but that He loved us and sent His Son as an atoning sacrifice for our sins... We love because He first loved us (1 John 4:10, 19 NIV).

I had the concept of love backwards. I thought that I loved so that God would love me. No. Love is not that I love God, but that He loves me, and He loved me first. If I don't receive His love first, then I have no ability, or Source, to love Him, myself, or anyone else.

In order to receive His love, I first must believe what He says. I must trust Him. Then I must stop trying to love and let Him love me. I must simply relax and receive His love.
Remember: 'Receive' is another word for 'faith." The very act of going to Him and accepting His love proves that I believe Him. Faith is an action word. You have to act on what you say you believe, or it is not faith. And without faith, it is impossible to please God.

He does not need anything from us. He doesn't need us to do anything for Him. He simply wants us to trust Him and believe (cling to, trust in, rely upon, put your whole weight upon) what He says is true. It is that simple.

I Cannot Love You If I Need You

Now get off your high horse and listen to me for a minute. Think about this.

Love is freedom. If I truly love you, I will give you freedom to choose. You can be and do whatever you want. Love wants only the best for you, not for me. Love is 'other-focused,' not 'self-focused.'

Agape love, God's unconditional love, means "giving of yourself sacrificially to meet the needs of another, not expecting anything in return."

Love meets someone else's needs, not its own. All God's needs are met within Himself. All our needs are met in Jesus. If we don't trust Jesus to meet our love needs, then we have to get them met somewhere else. That is an exasperating exercise in futility. No one can meet our needs but God.

When we 'need' someone to meet our needs, freedom turns into control. If I give you freedom to choose, you may not choose to meet my needs. Therefore, I have to manipulate and control you so that you meet 'my' needs. I'm not loving you (giving you freedom). I'm controlling you for selfish gain.

Dr. Larry Crabb gives a wonderful illustration in his great book, *Inside Out*. I highly recommend it to you.

The Fallen Pyramid vs. the Fruitful Pyramid

After the fall, Adam and Eve became the 'source' of meeting their needs. They did not trust God anymore so they stopped coming to Him as their 'Source.' They started looking out for #1. They needed something from each other, but they were too selfish to share.

Dr. Crabb says that married couples who don't love each other with God's love are "two ticks with no dog." I love that. The essence of love is 'giving,' not 'getting.' For God so loved the world that He GAVE...

The Fallen Pyramid

The foundation of this pyramid: I do NOT trust God.

God is the only Source who can meet my needs. If I do not trust God, and I refuse to go and get my needs met from Him, then I need YOU, not God, to meet my needs.

Since you cannot meet my needs because you don't have it in you, I get mad at you when I can't manipulate you to do what I 'need' you to do. As a matter of fact, I hate you.

When I hate you, the devil condemns me and tells me what a lousy Christian I am. He tells me there has to be something wrong with me, or else you would meet my needs. Then I begin to hate me for being such a louse.

At this point, I come to a crisis of belief that requires faith and action. What am I going to do? Am I going to throw myself on the mercy of God and go back to trusting Him as my 'Source,' or am I going to try harder to control and manipulate you?

If I don't go back to trusting God, I just have to try to survive my way. And here's how I will do it. I will become a master people-pleaser. I will try other tactics in order to coerce you into meeting my needs. And the cycle starts all over again.

The Fruitful Pyramid

When I get tired of beating my head against the wall trying to survive on my own, I decide to go back and start trusting God as my 'Source' to meet my needs. I take Him at His Word.

And my God will meet all your needs according to His glorious riches in Christ Jesus (Philippians 4:19 NIV).

In Christ, I have no needs. He IS everything I need. I need nothing outside of Him. Since He has no needs, and I am ONE with Him, then I have no needs either.

Now I don't need you to meet my needs. Now I can love you. I can release you to live free apart from my control and manipulation. Love is freedom. If you choose not to meet my needs in my way, I'm still okay. All my needs are met in Jesus.

Now do you understand why you cannot love someone from whom you need something?

Here is how the Fruitful Pyramid plays out:

I trust God as the 'Source' of all my needs. I need nothing from no one but Him. Then, and only then, am I free to love you. When I don't need anything from you anymore, then I can truly love you.

If you choose not to meet my needs in the way I want, I still accept you. I don't hate you. I accept you as God accepts me... unconditionally.

But sometimes, the 'flesh' overcomes me, and I start to fall back on being my own 'source' for my needs. When that happens, instead of hating myself for being such a lousy Christian, I examine myself.

"Kenny, why are we frustrated? Have we stopped trusting God? Are we back to being the 'source' of meeting our needs? We better run to the Lord and tell Him. Then we need to get back to allowing Him to live His life in us, through us, for us, and as us."

Instead of trying to survive, I surrender. I tell the Lord that He is God, and I am not. Here is how I do that.

"Lord, I'm returning the stool of my heart back to you, its rightful owner. Please take care of my needs for me. Go back to loving people in me, through me, for me, and as me. Thank You, Lord."

Vines & Branches

I am the Vine; you are the branches. Whoever lives in Me and I in him bears much (abundant) fruit. However, apart from Me [cut off from vital union with Me] you can do nothing (John 15:5 AMP).

A vine 'produces' fruit. A branch 'bears' fruit. There is a difference. Branches cannot produce fruit. Branches are 'fruit hangers.'

The only responsibility the branch has is to stay attached to the vine. Detached from the vine, the branch dies. It dies the minute is departs the vine. It may look as if it is still alive for a day or so, but it withers and rots away.

We are alive IN Christ as long as we remain IN Him, and He remains IN us. Sin detaches us from His life. Like the branch, we may look as if we are alive, but we die spiritually (which is the only part of us that is eternal) the moment we are separated from Him.

Because of Adam's indiscretion in the Garden, all humanity was and is born detached from the vine (Jesus). We are dead in our sin separated from the Life of God. Just as a branch has no life apart from the vine sharing its life with the branch, we have no life in us apart from Christ sharing His life in, through, for, and as us.

In the Christian life, what is the fruit produced?

The fruit of the Spirit is love, joy, peace, patience, kindness, goodness, faithfulness, gentleness and self-control (Galatians 5:22-23 NIV).

A Christ vine produces the fruit of the Spirit. The very nature and character of Christ.

Notice that 'fruit' is singular, not fruits. It is ONE fruit, just as Christ is ONE. There is no love fruit apart from the others.

Jesus does not give us the fruit of peace. He IS our peace. If Jesus is our life, then we not only have His peace, we have His love, joy, patience, kindness, gentleness, faithfulness, meekness, and self-control. It is a package deal. Not sold separately.

The key to producing fruit spiritually is to remain attached to Jesus by faith. He does the producing. We provide the hanger.

Vessels and Beverages

What is the purpose of a container? The name gives it away. A container's purpose is to contain something. I know there are containers, vases and such, in art galleries that were made for looks, but we are talking about real life containers here.

I'm sure you have a favorite cup. Maybe two or more. I have my 'Cherish the JOurneY' cup from which I love to drink my cappuccino. I have my big Yeti that I take with me when I play golf in the summer heat. I have my little Yeti that contains my cappuccino I take to the office in the mornings. But what good is the container if it does not 'contain' anything?

The most important thing is what is in the cup (vessel). My big Yeti cost over thirty bucks. That is a lot of money for me to pay for a cup even though it is a great cup. It keeps my cappuccino hot for hours and my cold drink cold for 18 holes. But if there is nothing in the cup, it is useless.

We were created to be vessels for God. He created us so that He could express Himself to the world uniquely. Jesus came to seek and to save that which was lost. He chose to do it in, through, for, and as us.

As a vessel, we are empty if He is not in us. There is no life in anything but Him. If He is not IN us, we have no reason or purpose for existing. That is why we were dead in sin. He was not IN us. We had no life apart from Him.

Let's say you are stranded in the desert dying of thirst. You have a state of the art canteen, but it has no water in it. If you could choose, would you rather have the empty canteen, or a dirty paper cup filled with water? That's what I thought.

In that scenario, water is life for you. The kind of vessel that contains it is of no value. An empty vessel has no value apart from what it contains.

You and I are vessels of Living Water, Jesus, Himself. Think about that for a minute. We live in a world that is dying of thirst for Living Water. He has given us the honor and privilege of carrying Him to people so that He can quench their dying thirst for life. WOW!

Why is it that people in the world spend so much time on making their vessels look good when they contain no life inside? It's because man looks at the outward appearance, but God looks at the heart. What is on the inside is the most important thing to God.

What's in your vessel?

Pop the Top

 Take the common 16.9 ounce plastic water bottle filled with water. It is filled with thirst quenching H_2O. Even though you hold the bottle of water in your hand, it will not quench your thirst until something happens. You must 'pop the top.' The water cannot be released until you remove the cap.

Vessels are not meant to keep what it contains. Vessels hold its contents until it can be released. What good would it do to fill vessels and never release the contents? I put cappuccino in my Yeti so I can drink and enjoy it, not sit there forever. Even my Yeti won't keep it warm that long.

As vessels of the Lord, we were created to pour Him out. Then He refills us so we can pour Him out again, and again, and again. The Bible tells us to "be filled with the Spirit" (Ephesians 5:18). That does not mean one time only. It means to be 'continually being filled.' A never ending process.

Jesus told the woman at the well:

Jesus said, "Everyone who drinks this water will get thirsty again and again. Anyone who drinks the water I give will never thirst — not ever. The water I give will be an artesian spring within, gushing fountains of endless life" (John 4:13-14 MSG).

The cap represents our faith, or the lack thereof. Before the water can come into the bottle, the cap has to be removed. By faith we open our hearts and receive Him as our life.

Once the Living Water is IN us, He wants to be poured out of us into the world. The cap has to be removed so that He can be released. But not to worry, He is filling us back up as we are pouring Him out. He is a never-ending supply.

Is your bottle still capped? Have you opened your vessel and allowed Him to fill you? Or have you received Him, but now you won't release Him for fear of what the world may think of you?

You think about that.

Hand in Glove

My Bride, Wanda, loves yard work. I do a lot of digging for her. I always wear work gloves to avoid blisters. When I put my hand in those gloves, they work hard. When I take them off, they do nothing but lay there. While my hands are in them, they are doing what my hands are doing. Take them off, and they stop.

While taking a break one day, I told the gloves to go finish digging up some monkey grass. They just sat there. I begged them, and they just looked at me. Then they said to me, "Without you, we can do nothing."

No, I don't have talking gloves, but they can't do anything unless I slip my hands IN them. Then they can do whatever I do.

113

As children of God, we are like my gloves. Without Him doing His work IN us, we just sit there, too.

The only thing my gloves have to do is to open up and let my hand inside. Then I do the work in and through them. Just like Jesus when He slips His hands into ours.

Points to Ponder

- We are eternally, infinitely loved. We have a Father who loves us more than any other human being on this planet ever has or ever will.

- Everything about our life is in the Father's hands. Without God being the initiator of His work in us and the producer of change, there wouldn't be any significant change in our life.

- No matter what our circumstance, God means it for good. The universe is completely safe for us. Nothing comes to us---Jesus and me--- unless it first passes through God's loving hands. We have no reason to fear.

- We are born again into God's family. We are a new superior type of creation. A child of God. We are not the 'old self' we've always known.

- Even while we are here on earth, we are seated in Christ at the right hand of the Father. We are a unique, one-of-a-kind expression of Jesus.

- The entirety of our existence now depends upon our 'oneness with Christ.' We relax into this reality and receive it like a child. We have no life apart from Christ. We have His life, and we are identical to Him in nature and character.

- Nothing we do today will make God love us more, and nothing we do today will make God love us any less. Our behavior doesn't determine our identity. Our spiritual birth determines our identity.

- We are accepted and acceptable in Christ. God is not disillusioned with us because he had no illusions about us to begin with.

- God wants an intimate, personal relationship with us. That's why He made us ONE with Him and fused us into an inseparable union.

- Our sufficiency can only be found in Christ. We live 'from' God and not 'for' Him because He is our Source from which we live life.

Section Six: The Key to Unlocking the Mystery Is
FAITH

Preface: Awaken!

What I am sharing with you has been more wonderful and life changing for me than I could have ever imagined. My only regret is that it took so many years for me to 'get it!' It is nothing like religion ever taught me. My awakening is a gift from the Lord which He offers freely to anyone who will receive it. Whether you choose to accept, or not, is entirely up to you.

One thing I have come to understand is that I cannot live beyond what I believe. If what I believe is a lie, then that is how I will live. And I lived a lie for many years until the Lord set me free.

I remember a season in my journey with the Lord where it was all about me trying to get more of Jesus, getting filled and refilled with the Spirit. It was all about continually thinking and doubting: Am I being good enough? Am I sinning? Am I not sinning?
Thanks be to God, I don't live there anymore! If that's where you are currently living, you must be completely exhausted and overwhelmed!!

Our (Jesus and me) goal for this book is to help you understand what it means for Christ to be your life, and what it looks like for Christ to live His life in you and through you. This life is nothing like 'religion' has ever taught you. Religion is death inducing. The truth is life-transforming!

The simple truth of 'Christ IN you' has been buried under a counterfeit gospel that manipulates believers into behaving like Jesus by keeping the rules. When you are uncertain of your true identity in Christ, you will begin to lean on your own effort. "Do this to get that blessing," or "Don't do this and stay free." It sounds reasonable, but it leads us away from dependency on Christ and teaches us to trust in ourselves. We may be justifying it by telling ourselves that we're co-laboring with God, but the true gospel is…

Jesus + Nothing = Everything

Our true Christian identity has been hidden in plain view since the writings of the apostle Paul; however, there needs to be a paradigm shift in order for us to 'get it' and especially to 'live it.'

So get ready to understand your true identity in Christ. Because of God's great love for you, it was His plan from eternity past to be joined with you forever. You were created for oneness and union with God.

You need to wake up to your new life, to possess it, to put it on. You need to realize your need to wake up from the stupor of religion. Realize you are born again into God's family. You are a new superior type of creation. A child of God. You are not the old you you've always known. That old you is gone forever.

Our goal is to take the jigsaw pieces and put them all together so you can plainly see how simple and wonderful your life IN Christ really is.

The penny that needs to drop for you is the understanding that you have no life apart from Christ. You have His life. As He is in heaven, so are you on earth. You and Jesus are identical in nature and character because He is your life. The old you does not exist anymore. The enemy will lie in order to hide the truth from you. Don't get to heaven and find out you have lived a lie.

All through the Bible, we find this common thread: **Christ IN you, the hope of glory.** This is the true mystery of faith! You still exist, but you are hidden IN Christ. Pray that the eyes of your heart will be enlightened to understand this mystery. God has given you the key to the Kingdom. All you have to do is unlock the door. The key is faith.

All the truth we have laid before you to this point means nothing if you do not act on it. Faith is not giving mental assent to some facts. It is acting on those facts. Faith is an action word.

There are mysteries in the realm of the spirit that will never be apparent to you. Jesus living in you is one of them. To the natural eye, it looks like you are living in you. When Jesus walked the earth, it looked like He was living on earth when in actuality it was the Father living His life through Jesus.

You might be asking, "So am I still me? Am I still alive, or is it Him?" You are still the unique 'you' God created 'you' to be, but Jesus is the Source of your life now. He expresses His life in you, through you, for you, and as you.

Are you ready? There is an amazing new life waiting for you. Awaken to it. All of creation is waiting. Jesus is waiting. What are you waiting for? Let's get started.

The Kingdom Is at Hand

When Jesus was thirty years old and began His official ministry, the very first thing He said was:

"Repent, for the Kingdom of Heaven is at hand"(Matthew 4:17 NKJV).

The Kingdom exists wherever God's children are in loyal submission to His will. There are two facets of His will which apply to every person on the planet.

1. To live in total dependence upon Him for everything we need.
2. To live in intimate and joyful relationship with Him enjoying life together.

Jesus Christ IS the Kingdom. In Him dwells the fullness of the Godhead bodily. Jesus stood before people and basically said, **"The Kingdom of God is at hand. It is standing right here in front of you. It is close enough for you to reach out and take it."**

They could not see Him as the Kingdom because they were looking at Him through the lens of religion. Even if some were not religious, they understood that God was 'religious.' The devout Jews of the day believed God was so holy that He dwelt in unapproachable light.

As a matter of fact, the religious sect of Jesus day would not even say the name of God out loud. They believed that speaking it would desecrate His holiness. Can you imagine what they thought when Jesus came along and said that they could call Father God, 'Papa?'

Since that first day Jesus began His earthly ministry, the Kingdom has been hidden in plain sight for everyone to see; however, they missed it because it was too obvious. People still miss it today because religion has told us that we have to work our way into the Kingdom when in reality, we are born into it as children of God. Jesus told the disciples:

"Let the children come to Me. Don't stop them! For the Kingdom of Heaven belongs to those who are like these children" (Matthew 19:14-15 NLT).

Two characteristics of children that please the Lord:

1. They are incredibly trusting. They believe anything they are told.
2. They are receivers, not givers.

That second one bothers you a little, doesn't it? Religion has taught us that it is better to give than to receive. But how can we give if we don't receive it to begin with? And do we have anything that we did not get from the Lord? We cannot give unless we first receive.

Receive is another word for 'faith.' When God tells us that He will meet our every need IN Christ, we prove that we believe Him by going to Him to receive it.

The Mystery Hidden in Plain Sight

"The obscure we see eventually. The completely obvious, it seems, takes longer" (Edward R. Murrow).

Jesus healed a man blind from birth in the ninth chapter of the Gospel of John. The religious elite were ticked off about it because it did not fit their theology. Jesus had healed this man on the Sabbath. They hunted the man down and interrogated him.

"What did this man, Jesus, do to you? How did He do it? No one sent from God would violate the Sabbath by working. Don't you know that this man is a sinner?" they shouted angrily.

To which the man replied, "Whether He is a sinner or not, I do not know. All I do know is this: Once I was blind, but now I can see!"

Jesus only denounced two groups of people. Those who heard him but did not believe Him and religious people. He denounced religion because it put obstacles and hurdles in the way of folks simply coming to Jesus by faith. Jesus hates anything that tries to separate us from Him.

Religion told me that Jesus plus obeying the law would save me.

Religion told me that Jesus plus good works would bring me blessings.

Religion taught me how to become a human 'doing,' not a human 'being.'

Religion told me that Jesus alone was not quite enough.

Religion told me I needed to try as hard as I could to be good, and what I couldn't do, Jesus would help me.

Religion deceived me for years. It obscured and covered over the obvious meaning of Scripture because it did not think life in Christ could be that simple. So religion tried to explain away the Good News.

Religion told me that I had to jump through the hoops of the little 'c' church to get to Jesus. The 'church' is the religious institution while the 'Church' is the true children of God who trust Him alone.

Skip the Middleman

I was saved years ago… born-again… gave my life to Jesus… confirmed… whatever your church background called it. Basically they told me that Jesus had forgiven me of my sins up to that point. But because I was human, I was still going to sin sometimes. Whenever I sinned, I needed to confess it to God and ask Him to forgive me for that sin.

In the meantime, I was supposed to do what Jesus would do. Doing it perfectly was the goal, but if I could not, then God would give me a little grace to help me through.

If you have listened to anything I have told you about eternal life being a Person, not a prize to attain, then you know the last paragraph is a lie. Jesus forgave ALL our sins… past, present, future… when we accepted His life as ours. We became ONE with Him. We have eternal life NOW, because Jesus IS eternal life. If He is going to live forever, then so am I because I live IN Him and He lives IN me.

For all who know Him as Lord, heaven is NOW because heaven for me is where Jesus will be. We don't have to wait to go to heaven when we die. We are there right now and can experience His life, joy, peace, love…. right this minute. He did everything FOR us. There is nothing left for us to do.

Grace means that He will give me what I need, when I need it. I cannot store up grace for the future in case I need it and God doesn't come through. He is dependable. He is my Source. I just live life and enjoy Him. I don't need a back-up plan.

I heard a story years ago that illustrates my point. I searched diligently for it and then I opened an old book the other day and there it was. The Lord found it for me. I want to share it with you.

An American businessman was on the pier of a small coastal Mexican village when he spied a small boat with just one fishermen in it. Inside the small boat were several large yellowfin tuna. The American complemented the Mexican on the quality of the fish and asked how long it took him to catch them. The Mexican replied, "It took only a little while."

The American then asked why he didn't stay out longer and catch more fish. The Mexican replied that he had enough to eat to meet his family's needs. The American then asked, "But what do you do with the rest of your day?"

The Mexican fisherman said, "I sleep late, play with my children, take a siesta with my wife, stroll into the village each evening where I sip some wine and play guitar with my amigos--- so I have a full busy life, Senor."

The American laughed and scoffed at him. He said, "You know, I have an MBA from Stanford. I can help you. You should spend more time fishing, and with the proceeds you could build a bigger boat, and with the proceeds from the bigger boat you could buy several boats. Eventually you would have a fleet of fishing boats, and then instead of selling your catch to that middleman over there, you could sell directly to the processor. Eventually you would be able to open your own cannery. You could control the product. You could control the market. You could control all the processing and distribution. And then, of course, you would need to leave this little fishing village and move to Mexico City. Then you would move to Los Angeles and eventually New York City, where you would run an expanding enterprise."

The Mexican fisherman said, "But, Senor, how long will this take?"

The American replied, "Maybe 15 to 20 years."

"But then what, Senor? What after 15 to 20 years?"

The American laughed and said, "That is the best part because after that, when the time is right, you could sell your company stock to the public and become filthy rich and make millions."

124

"Millions, Senor? What would I do then?

"Then you could retire and move to a small coastal fishing village where you could just sleep late, fish a little, play with your kids, take siestas with your wife, stroll into the village in the evening where you could sip wine and play guitar with your amigos."

Carpe diem. Seize the day. Live in the moment. Heaven is now. Skip the Middleman and go directly to Jesus.

I hope and pray that by the time we come to the end this book, you will be convinced and fully persuaded that truly...

Jesus + nothing = EVERYTHING

Andrew Farley says that Jesus contains no additives and needs no preservatives. He is all natural. Or should I say, supernatural.

All my life I believed that I was created to live for God. Now I know that God created me so that He could live FOR me. God opened my eyes as He did the man in the Gospel of John. And now I can see.

At long last, the mystery has been revealed to me. It was as if the scales fell from my eyes, and I could see it clearly. It was in plain sight the whole time.

I know you want to experience His life day by day. It is simple. It's just not easy.

It's simple because Jesus will live His life in you, through you, for you, and as you. Can't be anymore simple than that.

It is not easy because we like to be in control. The world has programmed us to be independent, but God created us to be dependent on Him and give Him control of our lives. The world, the flesh, and the devil will fight you tooth and nail to keep you from trusting Jesus to live FOR you.

But be not discouraged, Jesus has overcome them all. Keep believing!

'FAITH IT' Until You Make It.

I heard this phrase, FAITH IT, from my good friend, Bill Loveless. He has forgot more about grace than I will ever know. See for yourself. Check Bill out at www.christislifeministries.com

Religion focuses on behavior and feelings. Religion says that if you are not feeling it, 'fake it' till you make it. With religion, we have to 'fake it' because what it tells us is not reality.

In God's Kingdom, we don't have to fake it because He is reality. In our walk with the Lord, we 'FAITH IT' until we make it. That means we rely upon the truth of God's Word even when we don't feel it.

In our illustration above, FACT is the engine. The power source of the train. It represents the truth of God's Word.

FAITH is the coal car. It is the fuel that puts God's truth, the locomotive, into action. Although the FACT is true, we will not experience its power if we don't believe it and act on it.

FEELINGS ride along in the caboose. The caboose is empty. It has no power to pull the train. It is just along for the ride.

We are tempted to trust our feelings even though they cannot be trusted. Feelings arise from our thoughts. If our thinking is stinking and untrue, our feelings cannot distinguish the difference. For example, if I throw a rubber snake on you, you can die of heart attack because you think the snake will bite you. A rubber snake cannot bite you, but your feelings are unable to distinguish between what is real and not real.

The 'belt of truth' in the armor of God covers our waist. Long ago people believed that our emotions resided in the bowels. That is why the Bible talks about 'bowels of mercy' and 'bowels of compassion.'

God tells us to put on the 'belt of truth' so that our emotions are filtered through the truth and are not based on lies which can negatively affect our decisions. He knows that many of our decisions are based more on our feelings than the facts.

To experience His life IN us, we trust Him without regard to our feelings. Feelings can lie. He IS truth. He cannot lie. Therefore, we FAITH IT (trust and act on what God says) until our feelings line up with the truth.

The more we walk in faith (above the line), the more we 'experience' Him in our soul (below the line). As we keep FAITHING IT, our 'above the line' and 'below the line' experience merges and lasts longer and longer. Dennis Jernigan says that he wants to live in such unity with Christ that when he dies, he won't even notice the change. Wouldn't that be great?

Eternal/Spirit/I Am

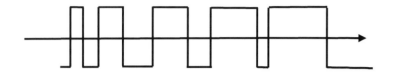

Temporary/Soul/I Am Becoming

'FAITHING IT' means that we continue to believe that God is working even though we are not feeling Him working in us and through us.

Let's assume that you are struggling with loving someone you are not particularly fond of. Now, if you cannot think of anyone, put this book down now and go love the world to life. The world needs you out there. You don't need to read this book.

Okay, that's what I thought. Let's continue.

A step of faith might look like this, "Lord, I cannot love this person. I am trusting You to love this person through me and for me."

Early on in this process, you are not feeling, or experiencing Christ's love. However, if you are walking by faith, FAITHING IT, what do we know is true?

Christ is constantly loving through you, in you, and for you. Since at this point you are not experiencing Christ's love, we call this a 'faith' love as Bill Loveless calls it.

If you continue FAITHING IT, then you will eventually come to a place where you will begin to 'experience' Christ's love for this person. His love will become real in your soul, not just in your spirit.

Remember that moving from faith to experience is a supernatural work of the Spirit that may take time. Be patient. Patience is a fruit of the Spirit. You have it in Jesus. He delights in doing everything FOR you. You are not bothering Him. However, it does bother Him when you don't trust Him to live FOR you.

Corrie Ten Boom Forgives Her Captor

It was in a church in Munich that I saw him—a balding, heavyset man in a gray overcoat, a brown felt hat clutched between his hands. People were filing out of the basement room where I had just spoken, moving along the rows of wooden chairs to the door at the rear. It was 1947 and I had come from Holland to defeated Germany with the message that God forgives.

It was the truth they needed most to hear in that bitter, bombed-out land, and I gave them my favorite mental picture. Maybe because the sea is never far from a Hollander's mind, I liked to think that that's where forgiven sins were thrown. "When we confess our sins," I said, "God casts them into the deepest ocean, gone forever."

The solemn faces stared back at me, not quite daring to believe. There were never questions after a talk in Germany in 1947. People stood up in silence, in silence collected their wraps, in silence left the room.

And that's when I saw him, working his way forward against the others. One moment I saw the overcoat and the brown hat; the next, a blue uniform and a visored cap with its skull and crossbones. It came back with a rush: the huge room with its harsh overhead lights; the pathetic pile of dresses and shoes in the center of the floor; the shame of walking naked past this man. I could see my sister's frail form ahead of me, ribs sharp beneath the parchment skin. "Betsie, how thin you were!"

[Betsie and I had been arrested for concealing Jews in our home during the Nazi occupation of Holland; this man had been a guard at Ravensbruck concentration camp where we were sent.]

Now he was in front of me, hand thrust out: "A fine message, Fräulein! How good it is to know that, as you say, all our sins are at the bottom of the sea!"

And I, who had spoken so glibly of forgiveness, fumbled in my pocketbook rather than take that hand. He would not remember me, of course—how could he remember one prisoner among those thousands of women?

But I remembered him and the leather crop swinging from his belt. I was face-to-face with one of my captors and my blood seemed to freeze.

"You mentioned Ravensbruck in your talk," he was saying, "I was a guard there." No, he did not remember me.

"But since that time," he went on, "I have become a Christian. I know that God has forgiven me for the cruel things I did there, but I would like to hear it from your lips as well. "Fräulein," again the hand came out—"will you forgive me?"

And I stood there—I whose sins had again and again to be forgiven—and could not forgive. Betsie had died in that place— could he erase her slow terrible death simply for the asking?

It could not have been many seconds that he stood there—hand held out—but to me it seemed hours as I wrestled with the most difficult thing I had ever had to do.

For I had to do it—I knew that. The message that God forgives has a prior condition: that we forgive those who have injured us. "If you do not forgive men their trespasses," Jesus says, "neither will your Father in heaven forgive your trespasses."

I knew it not only as a commandment of God, but as a daily experience. Since the end of the war I had had a home in Holland for victims of Nazi brutality. Those who were able to forgive their former enemies were able also to return to the outside world and rebuild their lives, no matter what the physical scars. Those who nursed their bitterness remained invalids. It was as simple and as horrible as that.

And still I stood there with the coldness clutching my heart. But forgiveness is not an emotion—I knew that too. Forgiveness is an act of the will, and the will can function regardless of the temperature of the heart. "Help!" I prayed silently. "I can lift my hand. I can do that much. You supply the feeling."

And so woodenly, mechanically, I thrust my hand into the one stretched out to me. And as I did, an incredible thing took place. The current started in my shoulder, raced down my arm, sprang into our joined hands. And then this healing warmth seemed to flood my whole being, bringing tears to my eyes.

"I forgive you, brother!" I cried. "With all my heart!"

For a long moment we grasped each other's hands, the former guard and the former prisoner. I had never known God's love so intensely, as I did then. (excerpted from "I'm Still Learning to Forgive" by Corrie ten Boom. Reprinted by permission from *Guideposts* Magazine. Copyright © 1972 by Guideposts Associates, Inc., Carmel, New York 10512>).

Why We Struggle with 'Faithing It' Long Enough

1. We live in a culture of INSTANT gratification.

One reason that we struggle with FAITHING IT is that we live in a society of instant gratification that says, "I want it, and I want it now!" We live in a 'microwave' culture that is often at odds with our 'crockpot' Lord.

We bring that same mindset into our walk of faith. We want to experience change and experience it quickly. But our faith walk is a marathon, not a sprint. It may take some length of time before you 'experience' transformation even though you are, indeed, transformed in Christ.

I believe that this is the #1 reason why most Christians never experience supernatural transformation. We want to experience change so quickly we are unwilling to take enough steps of faith in order to 'experience' change.

That is why the key question concerning your walk of faith is this: Will you 'FAITH IT' long enough to 'experience' transformation?

What if a baby takes its first step, maybe two, and falls down. What would you think if he said, "Well, looks like I'm not going to be able to walk? I tried and couldn't do it." And he never takes another step.

Ridiculous, right? He keeps trying to walk until one day you tell him, "Stop running in the house!" I guess he didn't give up, and neither should we.

2. satan will tempt you to QUIT walking by faith.

The last thing that satan wants is for you to comprehend that Jesus is your life and start believing it. As you are FAITHING IT, he will tempt you to quit your faith walk by inserting thoughts of discouragement and doubt. During the FAITHING IT period, remember to draw upon Christ's patience and perseverance until you experience change.

Don't Ever Lose Hope

Holding onto hope is part of our DNA. God created hope to interact with every facet of our lives. The Bible says that **"hope deferred makes the heart sick"** (Proverbs 13:12).

The essence of depression is hopelessness. A psychiatrist told me that the first question he asks a depressed patient is: "What are you going to do when you get over this?" The reason they are depressed is because they have lost hope. They believed the lie that they were never going to get better.

Why are you downcast, O my soul? Why so disturbed within me? Put your hope in God, for I will yet praise Him, my Savior and my God. My soul is downcast within me; therefore I will remember You (Psalm 42:5-6 NIV).

Jesus is our Blessed Hope!

Florence Chadwick loved to swim. She was born in San Diego, California on November 9, 1918. She grew up on the beach and began competing as a swimmer at the age of six. After four years of defeats, her uncle entered her in a contest at the age of ten in a two and one half mile "rough water" night swim where she came in fourth.

One year later at age eleven Chadwick won first place in a six-mile race across the choppy waters of the San Diego Bay Channel in her home town. For the next 19 years she continued as a competitive swimmer. When she was 13 she came in second at the U.S. national championships. She was the first woman to swim across the English Channel... both ways. She even swam across the Straits of Gibraltar.

In 1962, after a career of swimming accomplishments, Chadwick was inducted by the San Diego Hall of Champions into the Breitbard Hall of Fame.

Chadwick was 34 years old on July 4, 1952, when she attempted to become the first woman to swim the 21 miles across the Catalina Channel from Catalina Island to Palos Verde on the California coast.

The weather that day was challenging because the ocean was ice-cold, and the fog was so thick she could barely see the support boats that followed her. The tides and current were against her. And, to make matters worse, sharks were in the area. But at daybreak she decided to go forward anyway, expecting the fog to lift in time.

Hour after hour she swam. The fog never lifted. Her mother and trainer followed her in one of the support boats encouraging her to keep going. While Americans watched on television other members of her support crew fired rifles at the sharks to drive them away. She kept going and going. At about the 15 hour point she began to doubt her ability to finish the swim. She told her mother she didn't think she could make it.

Unfortunately, at 15 hours and 55 minutes she had to stop and with huge disappointment she asked her support crew to take her out of the water. Because of the fog, she could not see the coastline so she had no idea where she was. She soon found out, however, that she was less than a mile from the coast. She could have certainly reached it if she had just stayed in the water a few minutes longer.

Later she told a reporter, "Look, I'm not excusing myself, but if I could have seen land, I know I could have made it."

Indeed, she did make it. Twice, as a matter of fact, under the same adverse conditions. She said she could see the shore in her mind's eye this time and just kept swimming.

Do you see how strong the connection is between hope and faith? Think about it. You cannot have one without the other. Hope is the feeling that what is wanted can be had, or that events will turn out for the best. Hope is the foundation of our faith just as faith is the foundation of our hope.

Faith is the substance of things hoped for... (Hebrews 11:1).

'FAITH IT' until you make it!!!!! Don't ever give up!!!!

134

We live by the faith of the Son of God.

Now just so you know, it is not 'your' faith you are depending on. You don't have to struggle to muster up faith in your own strength. You even let Jesus 'believe' for you. It is His faith by which we live.

I have been crucified with Christ and I no longer live, but Christ lives in me. The life I live in the body, I LIVE BY FAITH IN THE SON OF GOD, who loved me and gave Himself for me. (Galatians 2:20-21 NIV, capitals mine).

Before the foundation of the world God chose us and placed us IN Christ (Ephesians 1:4). Jesus is the Lamb of God slain *before the foundation of the world* (Revelation 13:8).

How can that be? I thought Christ died on the cross two thousand years ago. How can He be slain before the world began?

God lives in the eternal NOW. God is outside of time. He is not limited by time. With God, everything is happening right now.

Placing you in Christ. Creation. The cross. The day you trusted Him as Lord and Savior. Right now while you are reading this book. Armageddon. It is all happening with God simultaneously. God sees everything past, present, and future at the same 'time.' Mindboggling? Absolutely!

Relax. We are not supposed to comprehend all this with our finite minds. It would be easier to teach a worm how to do brain surgery. That is why He is God, and we are not.

What I am trying to explain is why God created time for us and did not redeem our soul when He redeemed our spirit. God created man and gave him faith. All God has ever wanted from us is our trust. If we choose to trust Him, He will do exactly what He promises. If we don't trust Him, He is not pleased with our obedience no matter what we do.

Now faith is the evidence of things NOT SEEN... Hebrews 11:1 KJV).

135

God sees the future before it ever happens. If we could see what's going to happen, faith could not exist. It would be sight. Seeing is not believing. And faith is the evidence of things not seen. Understand?

God says, **"You cannot see what is going to happen tomorrow, but I can. Do you trust Me?"**

And it is impossible to please God without faith. Anyone who wants to come to Him must believe that God exists and that He rewards those who sincerely seek Him (Hebrews 11:6 NLT).

Faith is believing something is, even though it's not, so it can be, because God said it was. To put it another way, faith is believing something's so, even though it's not so, so it can be so, because God said it is so.

Allow me to destroy your faith.

Suppose I reach into my pocket and pull out an object. I conceal its identity by clenching my fist around it. I then tell you that I have something in my fist. I ask if you believe me. You affirm that you do. You put your faith in what I tell you.

Then I tell you that the object is a key and ask you again if you believe me. Again you affirm that you do. You are FAITHING IT. Then I open my hand and reveal to you the key. Your faith is destroyed because you don't need it anymore. You have sight.

Faith ceases to be faith if the object upon which you are placing your faith is seen. In God's economy, seeing is not believing. Believing (faith) comes before seeing. As the verse above says, **"faith perceives as real fact what is not revealed by our senses."**

Does God exist? How do you know? Can you see Him? Can you feel Him? Can the existence of God be verified by our physical senses, or by our intellect? No.

When Jesus says: **"I am the way and the truth and the life. No one comes to the Father except through Me** (John 14:6

NIV), we believe Him. And when we do, He becomes the way, the truth, and the life FOR us.

God reveals Himself to us when His Spirit unites with our new human spirit. Our soul makes the decision as to whether we act upon what God says in the spirit realm is true, or not. It is a matter of faith. The soul cannot 'see' into the spirit realm. It can only see through the faith eyes of the Spirit.

Our soul is like Susie, the blindfolded horse. Susie did not need to see with her soul and senses because she trusted the fact that her master could see where they both were going.

The Holy Spirit sees where we are going as well, and He communicates the directions to our soul. Are we going to trust our Master as much as Susie trusts hers?

One day when we leave the planet by death, or by His coming again, we will see Jesus face to face. Then our faith will be made sight. And we will no longer need faith. Until then, we keep FAITHING IT until we make it.

Biblical Faith Is an Action Word

Now the kind of faith that pleases God requires action. No, it is not based on what you DO. It is based on how you respond to what you say you believe. Biblical faith is an action word.

Biblical faith means 'cling to, trust in, rely upon, put your whole weight upon.' Merely saying that you believe something is just mental assent, not true Biblical faith. You must act on what you say you believe if you are to 'experience' the truth.

The Ten Lepers

As He entered a village there, ten lepers stood at a distance, crying out, "Jesus, Master, have mercy on us!"

He looked at them and said, "Go show yourselves to the priests." AND AS THEY WENT, they were cleansed of their leprosy (Luke 17:12-14 NLT, capitals mine).

In Old Covenant times, when a person was cured of a skin disease, he had to go to the priest for inspection and have the priest declare him clean. Jesus did not tell them they were healed. He simply told them to go see the priest as if they were already healed. Their healing was contingent upon their acting on what Jesus told them.

While they were standing there, they were not healed. They were healed only when they took off to see the priest. Faith is always an ACTION word. Faith is not true faith until it is ACTED UPON.

Three Aspects of Faith

In our soul, there are three aspects of faith:

- Mental--- what the mind thinks, often called, 'mental assent.'
- Emotional--- what we are 'feeling' which is determined by what we are thinking.
- Volitional--- what we choose to do by exercising our 'will.'

Take a look at this chair. Does it look sturdy enough to hold you up? If so, you have mental assent. You believe it will hold you up. But that is not true biblical faith.

If you stand for ten hours looking at it, you begin to wish and hope that it can hold you up. You are 'feeling' it by this time. But that is still not biblical faith.

By now, you believe it will hold you up, and you really want it to hold you up, but is it holding you up? No. Why not?

You have not exercised the most important aspect of faith.

Volitional. Your will. You have not acted on what you say you believe.

The chair will only hold you up if you act on what you say you believe. You have to sit in the chair. You have to 'put your whole weight upon it' before your faith is verified. The act of sitting on the chair is true, biblical faith. Now the chair is doing what it was designed to do and proves our mental assent.

That is why so many people are not 'experiencing' the love, joy, and peace of Christ. Oh, they believe He is all that. They truly want Him to be that for them. But they have never 'clung to, trusted in, relied upon, put their whole weight upon' what they say they believe.

Listen. I promise you this. If you take Jesus at His word, and act on what He says is true, you will experience in your soul what is already a fact in your spirit.

You are unconditionally loved in Christ. If you go out and live as if you are, you will experience it in your soul. You have to act on what you believe, or else you have no true faith. True faith requires you to do something about what you say you believe.

Raiders of the Lost Ark

Did you see the Indiana Jones movie, ***Raiders of the Lost Ark***? Remember when Dr. Jones came to a great chasm that separated him from the Holy Grail? His map said that there was a bridge across the chasm. Dr. Jones saw no bridge. Bad people intent on killing him were rapidly approaching from the rear. There had to be a bridge, or else he was dead.

When he reached out to tap the invisible bridge with his foot, there was no bridge. All he had to rely on was the map which said there was a bridge for those who would take 'a leap of faith.'

If he stayed there, he was dead for sure. If he stepped out and there was no bridge, he was still a dead man. The only hope he had was in the reliability of the map. He decided to take the 'leap of faith.'

When Dr. Jones stepped out onto the invisible bridge with all his weight, the bridge appeared out of nowhere. It did not appear when he was toe tapping (mental assent). It only showed up when he totally trusted what the map told him.

Faith is only as reliable as its object. The Bible is the owner's manual for living a meaningful life the way God intended. It is more reliable than Dr. Jones' map. The truths contained in Bible will work if we are willing to act on what it says.

Frozen Lakes

A frozen lake with ice a foot thick will hold you up no matter how scared you are if you only have enough faith to take one step. The OBJECT of your 'little faith' is fully reliable.

However, if the ice is only half an inch thick, it won't hold you up no matter how much faith you have. The OBJECT of your 'whole lot of faith' is not reliable at all.

The OBJECT of your faith is way more vital than the 'amount' of faith you have. Jesus said all the faith we need is the size of a mustard seed which is no bigger than a speck of dust.

Jesus Upset with His Disciples

At the foot of the mountain, a large crowd was waiting for them. A man came and knelt before Jesus and said, "Lord, have mercy on my son. He has seizures and suffers terribly. He often falls into the fire or into the water. So I brought him to your disciples, but they couldn't heal him."

Jesus replied, "You faithless and corrupt people! How long must I be with you? How long must I put up with you? Bring the boy to Me." Then Jesus rebuked the demon in the boy, and it left him. From that moment the boy was well.

Afterward the disciples asked Jesus privately, "Why couldn't we cast out that demon?"

"You don't have enough faith," Jesus told them. "I tell you the truth, if you had faith even as small as a mustard seed, you could say to this mountain, 'Move from here to there,' and it would move. Nothing would be impossible" (Matthew 17:14-20 NLT).

Jesus seemed a little upset with His disciples. Why?

Then He appointed twelve of them and called them His apostles. They were to accompany Him, and He would send them out to preach, GIVING THEM AUTHORITY TO CAST OUT DEMONS (Mark 3:14-16 NLT, capitals mine).

Jesus had given them the power and authority to cast out demons.

They did not believe Him, or else they could have cast out the demon.

I've said before that the only people Jesus denounced was religious people, but there is another group that raised His ire as well. Those who did not believe what He told them. On more than one occasion Jesus rebuked His disciples for their lack of faith.

Why do you call me, 'Lord, Lord,' and do not do what I say? (Luke 6:46-47 NIV).

Jesus' Hometown

But Jesus said to them, "Only in his hometown and in his own house is a prophet without honor."

And He did not do many miracles there BECAUSE OF THEIR LACK OF FAITH (Matthew 13:57-58 NIV, capitals mine).

Is Jesus implying that He would have done more miracles if they simply believed Him? I believe so.

Faith means "to cling to, trust in, rely upon, put your whole weight upon" the object of your faith.

Until we act on what we believe, what we call faith is merely 'mental assent.' Mental assent is the reason Billy Graham said that 80% of people on church membership rolls are lost.

Stand up in any Christian church and ask these questions:

- o Do you believe Jesus is the Son of God?
- o Do you believe He died on the cross for your sins?
- o Do you believe He rose from the dead?

How many hands do you think would go up? Every single one. Everybody in the church would say that they 'believed' that.

They think what they have is faith, but in reality, they are only giving mental assent to the facts.

The devil believes every one of those statements are true as well. And he trembles in fear just thinking about it (James 2:19 NKJV). And the devil is certainly not on his way to heaven.

Most people think that if they 'believe' in God, then they are Christians. NO! They are not.

Biblical faith means that you are trusting Christ to forgive your sins and to be your life FOR you because you are dead in sin.

Until you take that 'leap of faith,' Jesus will not become your life. I'm talking about "sink or swim, live or die, come hell or high water, I'm trusting Jesus." If He is lying, I'm dying. But He is not lying. He cannot lie. He IS the Truth.

We have spent a lot of time talking about FAITH and rightly so. The truths in the previous sections will mean nothing to you if you don't understand what biblical faith is. You will not be able to experience the life-transforming Truth of Christ living IN you if you don't understand that faith is an 'action' word.

Jesus, the OBJECT of our faith, is faithful and true. And He is waiting for you to take Him at His Word. You cannot walk on the water if you don't get out of the boat.

He has given you His Word: **"Come!"** Will you step out and take that 'leap of faith?' Take it from one who has taken the leap. You are about to embark on the adventure of a lifetime. I'm so excited for you.

Points to Ponder

- The Key to the Kingdom is FAITH.
- The result of our life lived by faith in Christ results in changes in our thinking, beliefs, behavior, and our choices.
- When we trust Christ to BE those things we need, that step of faith releases God's power, and we receive the fullness of Christ's life (all of His peace, strength, unconditional love, etc.) in that moment.
- Whether or not we feel or experience Christ's life in the moment when we ask for it, we know by faith that He is supplying His peace, patience, etc. and we will eventually experience the transformation that God promises.
- As we experience these changes, God will produce in us a God-confidence.
- Transformation is a life-long process. It is a journey, not a sprint. Our soul is continuously being transformed to believe the truth.
- Trust is the fruit of our growing confidence in God's love for us.
- Christ didn't come to help us live the life. He came to live it IN us!
- Biblical belief is an action word.
- Biblical belief means, "cling to, trust in, rely upon, put your whole weight upon."
- If you don't act on what you believe, your faith is not true faith. All you have is mental assent.
- Believing always precedes seeing.
- Faith is the fuel that makes the Fact of God's Word experiential.
- Your spirit has been made perfect in Christ.

- Your body and soul have not been made perfect... yet.
- When your soul surrenders to and trusts the truth in your spirit, your soul will begin to 'experience' what is true in your spirit.
- Until that happens, 'FAITH IT' until it happens. Don't ever quit!
- Step into the water. He is waiting for you.

Section Seven: Epilogue

Final Thoughts

If it sounds too good to be true, it probably is. I've heard that all my life, and 99.9% of the time it is true. Now when I hear something that sounds too good to be true, I say, "It must be Jesus." He is too good to be true, and yet He is.

Now that you have finished the book, if you don't think Jesus is too good to be true, I did a lousy job explaining how good He really is. He is more than wonderful. He is everything He says He is and so much more.

When I was trying to live 'a' Christian life, it was anything but abundant. I asked Jesus on many occasions: "Lord, where is the abundant life You said You came to give us? All I'm experiencing is exhaustion, discouragement, hopelessness, and despair. My life is anything but abundant."

Jesus has been pursuing me for years. All He ever wanted to do is love me and be abundant life for me. I went through some mighty dark days. Now I realize that He never left me for a second even though I was totally unaware of His presence most of the time. He is so faithful. He was just waiting for me to wake up, give up, and look up. When I did, He became more than too good to be true. He became everything to me.

Has He become everything for you? He is pursuing you, too, you know. Why don't you stop running and fall into His arms. You could use the rest. He knows how tired you are. He says so Himself.

"Are you tired? Worn out? Burned out on religion? Come to Me. Get away with Me and you'll recover your life. I'll show you how to take a real rest. Walk with Me and work with Me — watch how I do it. Learn the unforced rhythms of grace. I won't lay anything heavy or ill-fitting on you. Keep company with Me and you'll learn to live freely and lightly" (Matt 11:28-30 MSG).

Relax and let Jesus be the JOY in your JOurneY.

I know you still want to know how to DO that. Okay, here is how I DO that.

When I wake up in the morning, this is our conversation:

"Good morning, Lord. Thanks for the sleep. It was wonderful. Thanks for taking me with You and living FOR me today. I'm on Your agenda all day long. Let's not waste a minute. Since You are sitting on the stool of my heart, I know that wherever our journey leads us today is where You want us to go. Whatever I speak is what You want us to say. Whatever I see, is what you want us to see. Whoever we meet is who You want us to connect with. There will be no coincidences today. Everything that happens today has been orchestrated by You before the foundation of the world. WOW! Thank You for sharing this adventure with me. You are simply the best. I love you lots. Now let's go. I can hardly wait."

Then I get up and live. And live WE do! And so can you. No more analysis paralysis. Just living and loving IN Jesus.

Now that the mystery has been unlocked, what are you waiting for? It's time to step out of your comfort zone, and INTO His!

Kenny publishes a weekly dose of encouragement
each week called ***The Graceline.***

To join The Graceline Family, go to www.kennyashley.com
and enter your email address.

You can also visit www.Journey220.org to see and hear
Kenny's sermons, watch his vlogs, read his blogs,
and see all the great things Jesus is doing
in, through, for, and as us at
The Journey in Lake Wylie.

Go to Amazon.com to see Kenny's other books:

Waterholes in the Wilderness
Anchors in the Storm
Jesus, My Final Answer
Footprints of the Heart

Made in the USA
Middletown, DE
19 January 2022

59108132R00092